Ruth Marini
Dodger Ace

**RUTH MARINI
on the Mound**

Ruth Marini
Dodger Ace

Mel Cebulash

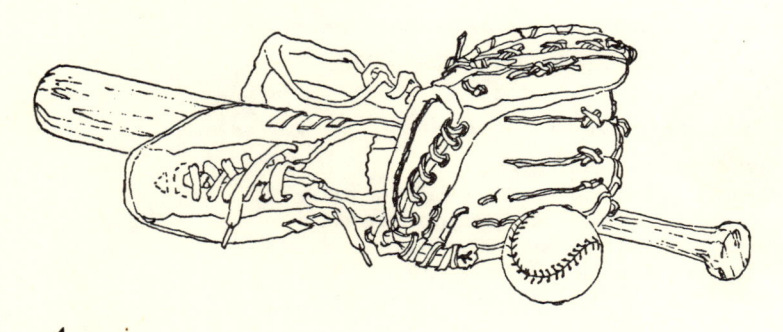

Lerner Publications Company • Minneapolis

Copyright © 1983 by Lerner Publications Company

All rights reserved. International copyright secured. No part of this book may be reproduced in any form whatsoever without permission in writing from the publisher except for the inclusion of brief quotations in an acknowledged review.

Library of Congress Cataloging in Publication Data

Cebulash, Mel.
  Ruth Marini, Dodger ace.

  (Ruth Marini on the mound)
  Summary: Ruth Marini becomes the first woman professional baseball player, advancing from the minor league to pitch for the Los Angeles Dodgers.
  [1. Baseball—Fiction] I. Title. II. Series.
PZ7.C2997Ru 1983   [Fic]   82-20383
ISBN 0-8225-0726-9

Manufactured in the United States of America

1 2 3 4 5 6 7 8 9 10 93 92 91 90 89 88 87 86 85 84 83

For my father, Jack Cebulash,
Remembering our Sunday walks to Weehawken Stadium

Ruth Marini
Dodger Ace

1

"Hey, are you Ruth Marini?" the man in the airplane seat next to Ruth asked.

Ruth was expecting the question. The man had been glancing over at her often during the hour since the plane had lifted off the runway at Newark Airport. "Yes, I am," she answered, hoping he wasn't going to ask how she felt about being the first woman to play big league baseball.

"Relax," the man said, smiling at her. "I know it's a long flight to LA, so I'm not going to drive you crazy with questions."

The man's warm smile put Ruth at ease. "I didn't mean to sound so uptight," she said. "I guess I am a little nervous."

"Well, I don't blame you," he said, extending his hand. "By the way, I'm Sal Surino. I live in LA."

Ruth was going to be living near the Dodger Stadium in a city called Glendale. She wasn't sure how close it was to Los Angeles. Sal Surino explained that Glendale was considered to be a part of LA along with a lot of other cities in Los Angeles County. He himself actually lived in Burbank, but he told people LA because it was more familiar.

In a way, Ruth understood. Her hometown of Union City, New Jersey, was just across the Hudson River from New York City, and some people liked to think of it as part of the greater New York metropolitan area. She liked to think of it as Union City.

"What made you decide to live in Glendale?" Sal Surino asked.

Ruth shrugged her shoulders. "I didn't decide. I'm going to be living with Karen Spillman. Her father is one of the Dodger executives. I met her down in Florida at spring training, and she offered to let me share her apartment if I made the team. She's around my age, and I think it'll be fun to room with her."

The conversation turned to Ruth's high school pitching days and then to last year—her first in professional baseball. Ruth was surprised at how much Sal knew about her record with Albuquerque. Because she was the only woman ever to play in the Pacific Coast League, she had received a lot of newspaper and TV coverage, but Sal sounded as if he knew much more than the average fan. "I guess I have a good memory," he explained.

Their conversation was interrupted by the service of drinks and food. Ruth ordered a Coke and Sal bought a martini. Thinking about calories, Ruth skipped the dessert of chocolate cake on her meal tray. During the week she'd spent at home, she'd gained about five pounds. She wasn't fat, but she wasn't in as good a shape as she had been at the end of spring training. She blamed her mother for the few extra pounds. Mrs. Marini had acted as if Ruth looked like a skeleton and had forced one meal after the other on her. Mike, Ruth's boyfriend, hadn't helped. He seemed to feel that they couldn't get through an evening without having a pizza or a sack of hamburgers from the local White Castle.

After the steward removed their trays, Sal said, "Wasn't I reading that you had some rough moments in spring training?"

"Not really," Ruth answered. "Except for the game with the Yankees, I pitched pretty well. The Yankees got to me, though. My curve was hanging and they clobbered it."

"I meant trouble with the players."

"Well, some of them did say some nasty things, but they're playing to win, and if rattling me will help, they're going to try it. I learned a lot about taking it last year. Even in high school, the other teams didn't like batting against a girl pitcher. I probably have had it easy compared to what I've heard happened to Jackie Robinson and some of the other black players who first broke the color thing in baseball. They even had trouble getting rooms in hotels."

"Well, Robinson had some of the same trouble you're having," Sal suggested. "Some of his teammates were rotten to him."

Ruth guessed that Sal was thinking about Tim Bender and Ralph Madden. They were Dodger pitchers who had made some of the remarks about her ability to pitch in the big leagues that had been reported in the newspapers. She especially disliked Bender because he'd been quoted as saying "baseball wasn't a game for girls, women, or old ladies." Madden hadn't gone that far, but he'd hinted that the Dodgers' sole purpose for having Ruth was to get big crowds at the games. Just thinking about the pitchers' remarks made Ruth's face turn red.

"I didn't mean to get you upset," Sal said. "Bender must be afraid of you, and I suppose Madden is, too."

"Maybe they are," Ruth said. "Bender used to be a great pitcher, but he's getting old. If things work right, I'll be one of the starting pitchers, and you know where that'll leave him."

"Madden had only a fair season last year."

"Yeah, I know," Ruth agreed. "He ought to be paying attention to his arm instead of talking about me. I just want to do the best I can for the team. You know what I mean? I don't have anything against anybody."

"Well, Madden had a couple of battles with the manager last year," Sal said. "I suppose he's that kind of guy. He cries a lot."

Ruth grinned. "He does act like a baby," she said, "but that's none of my business. I'm keeping my mouth shut and playing ball. We have a good team and I'm just glad to be on it."

"That's smart of you," Sal said. "I think you'll have a fine year."

Ruth closed her eyes. The food had made her a little sleepy. Minutes later, she fell into a sweet dream about being given the opening-day pitching assignment. She was three outs away from a no-hitter when the captain announced that the plane was beginning its descent into Los Angeles. Ruth glanced out the window. Below her, she saw miles and miles of buildings. It didn't look like New York, but it was huge. She wished she'd had time to finish her dream and she also wished it could come true.

The landing was smooth. Despite the steward's warnings, people jumped up and began taking their luggage from the overhead racks as soon as the plane was on the ground. Ruth smiled over at Sal. "I'm not in any hurry," she said.

"I just have a carry-on up front," he told her. "I hope I see you again sometime. I really enjoyed talking to you. Anyway, good luck. Everybody needs some good luck."

"Thanks," Ruth said, realizing she didn't know anything about him except that he lived in Burbank, wherever that was. "You, too. I'll look for you at the ball park."

Ruth watched Sal move off down the aisle. Time to go, she told herself, feeling excited about seeing Karen again and nervous at the same time.

Ruth spotted Karen in the crowd of people greeting passengers. She was wearing shorts and a halter and looked just the way Ruth expected a Californian to look. "Karen," Ruth called to her.

Karen hugged Ruth and told her how happy she was to see her. Ruth felt the same way. As she walked along with Karen to the baggage claim area, she thought of what it would be like if she were going to live alone in this big city. Ruth guessed it would be fun for some people, but she didn't think that she'd like it. She felt good around Karen and was sure they'd get along well.

Ruth had four pieces of luggage, so she got a redcap, who loaded the bags on his cart and followed Karen and her to the parking lot. It was hot, and the warm sun made Ruth think of the cold weather she'd left behind in New Jersey. "Is it always like this in the spring?" she asked.

"Sometimes it's warmer," Karen answered, "but I like it cool like this."

Ruth glanced over at Karen, wondering if she were kidding. She wasn't. "I can tell for sure I'm going to like the weather," she said.

"You'll like everything," Karen said, as they arrived at her car, which was a sharp blue Toyota with a liftback. After the redcap put the luggage in the back of the car, Ruth handed him two dollars. "Thanks," the man said, "and say, could you do me a little favor and sign this sheet of paper for my daughter? She's crazy about the Dodgers."

Ruth blushed as she signed the paper, and Karen laughed at her once she was settled in the car. "You're going to have to get used to being famous," Karen said, "or else you're going to be blushing all the time."

"Did you tell him I was on the Dodgers?" Ruth asked.

"I didn't have a chance to tell him. You saw that. The newspapers and the TV told him. Your picture is all over."

"Well, I guess I'd better get used to it," Ruth said. "The man sitting next to me on the plane even knew me. He was real nice. He was from Burbank. His name was Sal Surino."

"What?" Karen shrieked. "What did he look like?"

As best she could, Ruth described the man, and Karen nodded her head vigorously. "Did he ask you a lot of questions?" she asked.

"Not too many," Ruth answered, "but why? Who is he?"

"He's a sportswriter for the *Examiner*," Karen said, "and he doesn't make any secret about not liking the Dodgers. I'm sure glad he didn't ask you a lot of questions because if he did, you'd probably be reading your answers in the paper in the next few days and they might not sound so good after going through his typewriter."

Ruth thought of what she had said about Bender and Madden. "Karen," she confessed, "I think I've just gotten off to a bad start in LA—a very bad start."

2

Ruth loved Karen's apartment. She expected it would be nice, but she never imagined it would be as lovely as it was. The living room had a working fireplace and a small balcony that looked down on a huge swimming pool in the inner courtyard of the apartment complex. "It's too good to be true," Ruth told Karen.

"I'm glad you like it," Karen replied, "and I'm really happy you decided to room with me. I suspect some of my friends at college will come calling just to meet you, but I'll try to keep them away."

"Oh, don't worry about it," Ruth said. "I like talking to people my own age. I wouldn't want to meet any tonight, though."

Karen understood. Ruth had to report to practice the next morning, and Charley McGraw, the Dodgers' new pitching coach, was picking her up at seven. Charley had a special interest in Ruth. He had secretly coached her at his home in South Carolina, and on his recommendation, the Dodgers had signed her to a contract last year. It had been his suggestion that Ruth spend a season pitching for Albuquerque in the Pacific Coast League. Ruth had pitched well in the Coast League, and Charley finally felt she was ready for the Dodgers. He'd told her so at spring training and surprised her with the news that he had signed to be pitching coach. Ruth liked Charley and Sally, his wife, but she knew that their friendship wasn't going to influence Charley. If she didn't pitch well, she'd soon be back in Albuquerque.

While Ruth unpacked, Karen fixed a light dinner for the two of them. They talked while they ate, and both of them began to relax a little. They realized it was going to take a while to get to know each other. "You look exhausted," Karen said. "Why don't you just go off to bed. I'll take care of clearing the table."

"I think I will," Ruth said, realizing that her body was still running on Eastern time. "I'll see you in the morning."

"You won't see me," Karen called after her. "I don't have to get up that early, but give my best to Charley. He's a nice guy."

Charley was a nice guy, but the next morning was an exception. "I see you fattened up while you were home," he told Ruth as they walked to his car.

"I only gained about five pounds," she answered defensively.

"Five pounds overweight," Charley said. "When you left the training camp you were in shape. The Dodgers are paying you a fat salary, partly on my say-so, and I don't need any overweight pitchers on my staff. Do you understand that?"

"I heard you," Ruth said sourly, "and in case I forget, it's nice to see you."

Charley grinned. "Same here," he told her, handing over his car keys. "Now you drive."

"Are you kidding?" Ruth asked. "I'm not sure I'm ready for any freeway driving."

"Listen," Charley said, "I'm lending you this car until we see if you're sticking with the Dodgers. If you are, you'll have to buy a car because you can't get around LA without one. Now get behind that wheel and drive. The freeways are nothing compared to those potholed roads in New Jersey."

By the time Ruth pulled into a parking space at Dodger Stadium, she guessed she'd lost a couple of the pounds Charley had complained about. "I hope you remembered how you got here," Charley said. "Tomorrow you'll be doing it by yourself."

Ruth grinned. "I hope you're insured," she answered.

At the clubhouse entrance, Charley introduced Ruth to Sam Larkin, the clubhouse manager. "We have a dressing room and a shower all set up for you," Sam Larkin told her. "I guess you'd better come with me."

"Yeah," Charley said, "and, Sam, also point out the passageway to the playing field. I'll see you out there, Ruth, and don't bother wearing spikes. You're going to be doing a little running today."

Inside the dressing room, Ruth hurried over to look at her new uniforms, which were hanging on a clothes rack at one side of the room. She touched the blue letters that spelled out her name on the backs of the playing jerseys, and she looked at the number beneath her name. It was the "13" she had requested. "Is it true you wanted that number?" Sam Larkin asked.

"I sure did," Ruth said. "It's a lucky number."

"I hope it is for you," Sam said. "It wasn't for Ralph Branca."

"Who's Ralph Branca?" Ruth asked.

Sam smiled. "He was way before your time, young lady," he said. "He pitched for the Brooklyn team back in the forties. He was the guy who gave up that famous play-off home run to Bobby Thomson. He was wearing number 13 that day."

"Well," Ruth said, "all pitchers give up home runs. I'm not superstitious."

"I'm not either," Sam said, "but Branca was never the same after that home run. You do good and people will probably forget Branca wore that number. Anyway, most people aren't old enough to remember him or the home run. I've just been around longer than most people."

"I'll do the best I can," Ruth said, nodding at the short, white-haired man.

"I'm for you," Sam replied. "Now you get changed and follow the tunnel to your left. Just wear one of the training uniforms."

"I know," Ruth said.

"I thought you did," Sam said, winking at her, "but I know how you can forget things on your first day."

As Ruth changed, she wondered what Sam Larkin really thought about a woman playing for the Dodgers. From what he'd said, he'd probably been around when Jackie Robinson became the first black player in the big leagues. Someday, she'd ask Sam about Jackie Robinson. From what she'd read and heard about his treatment, her life in baseball seemed like a picnic so far. No, she thought, picnic isn't the right word, but Jackie Robinson had been treated terribly. He had been a brave man—much braver than Ruth imagined she could be.

When Ruth reached the playing area, she saw groups of players in different parts of the field. She headed for the group of pitchers huddled around Charley. "Hey, Ruth," a voice called to her.

She turned and saw Tommy Francona, the Dodger manager, trotting toward her. "Hi, Tommy," she said, as he shook her hand.

The stocky manager smiled at her. "You look all right," he said. "Charley told me that you put on a few pounds, but he'll get them off you. Too much pasta, kid?"

"And pizza and hamburgers and soda," she said, shrugging her shoulders, "but I didn't think it showed."

"Charley always had a good eye," Tommy admitted. "How's your arm?"

"I guess it's fine," Ruth said.

"Good. If Charley agrees, I'll let you start against the Angels on Friday. The game's in Anaheim."

"I know," Ruth said, feeling a sudden rush of nervousness about pitching against the Angels. They were regarded as the best team in the American League. Their pitching wasn't spectacular, but their hitters were murder. "I'd better get over with the pitchers," Ruth said.

"I'll see you later," Tommy said, slapping her on the back.

Most of the Dodger pitchers, including Tim Bender and Ralph Madden, greeted Ruth, but one just stared at her. That was Maury Jenkins. He'd just been traded from the Pirates, but Ruth recognized him from the pictures in the newspapers. He was in his mid-thirties, and he looked as mean as the papers said he was. He'd once been the best on the Pirates' pitching staff, but over the last few seasons, he'd lost as many games as he'd won. According to the papers, he hoped to get a fresh start with the Dodgers.

Ruth saved her warmest greeting for Ken Newton. He was a young black pitcher, and in spring training, he'd been friendliest of all the players to Ruth. This was his third year with the Dodgers, and last year he had won 14 games. As he had told her, he was getting better all the time.

"Maury," Charley said, "this is Ruth Marini."

"I would have never guessed," Maury answered, extending his hand to Ruth and smiling at the couple of guys who laughed at his line. "I'm Maury Jenkins, and I hope you'll excuse me for not tipping my cap."

Ruth didn't answer. She hadn't expected the remark, and she didn't like it.

"All right," Charley said, "now I'll tell the rest of the jokes. We're just going to work out easy today. Exercises, a little lobbing of the ball, and more exercises. Maybe we'll finish up with a little running."

The players groaned, and Charley grinned at them. "I'm happy to hear how much you like running," he said. "If you stay in shape, you won't have to do too much of it. The overweights will do more, while you're lobbing the ball around. For now, the overweights are Ruth and Maury. I don't think I need to tell the rest of you guys about the good Mexican food served in LA, but let me warn you that too much will have you running—on this field every practice session."

Everybody laughed except Ruth and, as she noticed, Maury. He looked angry.

Benny Green, Charley's assistant, took over and started the pitchers on some warm-up exercises. Then Charley started to walk away, and Maury followed him. Concentrating on the exercises kept Ruth from watching the conversation between Charley and Maury, but from what she could see, no friendly words were being exchanged. When Maury rejoined the group, his face was red and he looked angrier than before.

After the exercises, Benny Green told Ruth and Maury to circle the field a few times. He said if they did it too slowly, they could try a couple more turns. Because Maury was a veteran of training, Ruth fell in alongside of him. He was jogging at what seemed like a snail's pace to Ruth, but she guessed he knew how fast they had to go to satisfy Benny.

"What made you think you could play baseball with men?" Maury asked Ruth as they ran.

"What makes you think I can't?" she snapped back.

"I got a girl almost your age," he said, "but we raised her to be a lady. She doesn't chew tobacco and she doesn't play baseball."

"Good for you," Ruth said. "I wouldn't want her taking my place."

"*I'm* taking your place," Maury said. "I'm going to be a starting pitcher on this team, and I figure you'll be the easiest one to replace."

"That's your right," Ruth said, "but why don't we just wait and see what happens?"

"You wait," Maury said, and Ruth saw the unpleasant look that spread across his face. "I've been around baseball a long time. It's no game for girls. You may have been some kind of lucky freak in the Coast League, but the guys in the big leagues will run you back to that slum town you grew up in, and I'll really get a laugh out of that."

"Well, I'm glad about one thing," Ruth said, as she started to run ahead of Maury.

"What's that?" he called after her.

"That I'm not your daughter. I feel sorry for her."

Ruth didn't hear Maury's answer, but from the tone of his voice, she knew just about what he had to say. For the rest of the day, she steered clear of him, and she thought he might be staying away from her too. They weren't through with each other. She was sure of that, but she had other things to worry about.

3

Two days later, Ruth's extra pounds were gone. Charley credited the running for her quick loss of weight, but Ruth thought it was due to driving on the freeways. She guessed it would be quite some while before she felt comfortable on the roads to and from Dodger Stadium. Just remembering the directions burned up a lot of energy.

In practice, Ruth had begun throwing hard, and though her arm was a little sore, she was pitching well. Her fastball was hopping, and her control was good. "I'm going to tell Tommy you're ready to start the day after tomorrow," Charley told her. "You don't have any objections to that, do you?"

"No," Ruth said, happy with Charley's approval, "I can handle it."

"We'll see," Charley replied. "I want you to spend the rest of the day going over the Angels' batting order with Ernie."

Ernie Kirk was in his sixth year as the Dodger catcher. His hitting wasn't outstanding, but he was regarded by many sportswriters as one of the smartest catchers in the big leagues. Ruth soon learned why. One by one, Ernie reviewed each Angel starting player with Ruth. He told her where *not* to pitch to each of the players, except Ralph Jackman. "He's tough," Ernie told Ruth. "He hits good pitches and he hits bad pitches. The best thing to do is throw him slow stuff. That way, if he hits one out of the park, he'll be using his own strength. There's no sense in helping him with fast pitches. He's dangerous enough."

Ralph Jackman was in his mid-thirties, and he was a sure thing to make the Hall of Fame after he retired. He was third on the all-time home run list and though he didn't figure to break Hank Aaron's record, he was great. He'd been a big star when Ruth was in elementary school, and the thought of pitching to him thrilled her and made her nervous at the same time.

The other Angels were dangerous, too, but Ernie's tips gave Ruth a sense of confidence. She concentrated hard on everything he had to say. "Listen," he finally told her, "we'll go over it again tomorrow, and if necessary, you can take notes and study them tomorrow night. The key thing is going to be not to get rattled by the Angels or their fans."

"I'm not going to get rattled," Ruth answered defensively.

"Okay," Ernie shrugged, "but I'm on your side, kid. I just wanted you to know that I don't think you're in an easy spot."

"I'm sorry," Ruth said, realizing how she had sounded. "I know you're on my side."

That evening at dinner, Ruth told Karen about her

pitching assignment. Since her father had worked for the Dodgers for many years, Karen knew a lot more about baseball than a casual fan. Once the baseball season started, she was going to be working as an usher at the stadium, but for now, she was finishing her second year at Glendale Junior College. The next school year, she planned to transfer to Cal State at Northridge. It was a short drive, so she was going to keep her apartment. Ruth was happy about that because she liked her living arrangements and liked Karen.

"The Angels are really tough at home," Karen said, "but they're tougher on lefthanders than they'll be on you. I'm going to be watching the game on TV. I'm having a few friends over. I think they'd like to meet you sometime, but I guess they'll be gone by the time you get home."

"I'd love to meet them," Ruth said, "so don't chase them away even if I lose."

"I won't," Karen assured her, "but you're not going to lose. I'm sure of that."

"I'm glad you are," Ruth told her roommate and realized that she was becoming nervous about the game.

Later that evening, Ruth called Mike Garcia. Though it had only been a short time since she had left Union City, she missed Mike. The past summer, Mike had managed to get a job with his uncle in Albuquerque, and he and Ruth had become very close. Now they were separated again for a while, and they'd agreed that they would date other people. As Ruth dialed Mike's number, she hoped he wasn't out on a date because no matter how hard she tried, she would feel jealous.

Mike's "hello" relieved Ruth. "I just thought I'd check on you," she said jokingly.

"Oh, yeah," he said, joking back. "Well, it's late here. I just got home from a great date. I would have stayed out longer, but I was afraid you'd call."

Ruth laughed. "You're mean," she said, "and I was missing you."

"I miss you, too," Mike said, turning serious. "When I'm really feeling selfish, I wish you were back here in Union City working as a clerk in Mr. Levy's Insurance Company."

"I don't miss that office," Ruth replied.

"Well, what's happening?" Mike asked.

Ruth told him about her apartment, about driving to Dodger Stadium, and about her practice sessions. Then she informed him that she would be starting against the Angels on Friday night. "Watch out for Jackman," Mike said. "He can hit anything."

"I see you're still a catcher at heart," Ruth said. "Ernie Kirk gave me about the same advice this afternoon."

There was a silence on the other end of the line, and Ruth realized she'd touched a sensitive spot. Mike had been her catcher back in their playing days at Union Hill High School, and he'd dreamed of playing professional baseball. It was just a dream, but she guessed he still wished it had come true. "Hey," Ruth said, "if I were running the show, you'd be my regular catcher."

Mike laughed. "It's a good thing you aren't running the show," he said. "Ernie Kirk will be fine."

"He's a nice guy, and he really knows the batters. He ran through them with me this afternoon."

"They won't be broadcasting the game here," Mike said, "but I'll be hoping you win. If I get a chance, I'll call your mother and tell her, or did you already talk to her?"

"No," Ruth replied, "you call her if you can. I haven't been gone long enough to be homesick, but I did want to hear your voice."

They talked a while longer, but there really wasn't a lot to say. Still Ruth felt better when she put down the receiver. She loved Mike, and one of these days, she was going to come right out and tell him. He loved her, too. He hadn't said so yet, but his actions told her that he did.

When Ruth was changing for practice the next morning, the sound of someone knocking on the dressing room door surprised her. She pulled her Dodger Blue practice jersey over her head and called, "Come in."

It was Sam Larkin, the clubhouse manager. "The skipper wants to see you in his office," Sam said, pointing off down the corridor.

"The manager?" Ruth asked.

"Yeah, Tommy," Sam said, grinning at her question. "All you young ballplayers are the same. In the old days, everybody knew that 'skipper' was a nickname for the manager. I don't even know where the word came from, but it was used all the time. Nowadays, you and everybody else can't understand me. I must be getting old."

"You don't seem old to me," Ruth said with a smile.

"You're a nice kid," Sam said, "so hurry up now and get over to Tommy's office. He didn't look in one of his better moods."

"What does he want?" Ruth asked, showing her curiosity.

Sam winked at her. "I just work here," he said, "but don't you worry. He barks, but he doesn't bite."

Ruth laced her practice spikes and rushed off to Tommy Francona's office. "It's open," he called gruffly in answer to her knock.

"Did you want to see me?" Ruth asked, wondering if she should drop into one of the chairs opposite his desk.

"I sure did," he responded. "Sit yourself down and take a look at this, if you haven't seen it already."

Tommy Francona handed her a section of a newspaper. Ruth could see that it was the sports section of the *Examiner*, and though she hadn't read it, her thoughts jumped to her plane trip to Los Angeles and the man who had been seated next to her.

"No, I haven't seen it," she said, taking the paper and trying to remember the name of her traveling companion.

"Read Sal Surino's column—the second paragraph," Tommy told her.

The name rang a bell in Ruth's head. She quickly glanced at the paper and found "Sal Surino's Sideline Secrets." Her eyes moved to the second paragraph of the column and she read:

> *TRUE BLUE:* Met Ms. Ruth Marini the other day. Nice enough gal for a baseball player, but she's carrying a heavy chip on her shoulder. Seems she doesn't like Tim Bender and Ralph Madden. Seems the two gentlemen in question made some ungentlemanly remarks abut Ms. Marini's athletic abilities and about

29

women being in what has been a man's game. Now Ms. Marini probably has some constitutional right to be miffed, but she and the Dodgers probably will be better served if she saves her anger for the players on opposing teams. As for Bender and Madden, they have a few winning seasons to help prop open their big mouths.

Ruth set the newspaper on Tommy's desk. Her face was red and she knew it. "I gather there's a little truth in that column," Tommy said, "but what I don't understand is how you came to be talking to Surino. Can you explain that?"

"He was sitting next to me on the plane," Ruth said. "I didn't know he was a reporter. I thought he was a fan."

"That's worse," the manager roared. "Listen, we're a team here. If we have any problems, we don't lay them on the fans. We talk out our problems as a team. Now I spoke to Bender and Madden a couple of weeks ago. They were through mouthing off. They haven't bothered you since you arrived here, have they?"

"No," Ruth admitted, "they've been fairly friendly."

"Do you think they're going to be friendly now?" Tommy asked.

"Okay," Ruth said, "I made a mistake. What else can I say?"

"You can tell them," Tommy said.

"Oh, no," Ruth answered. "I'd like it to end, but they started it and they didn't tell me about any mistakes."

"Well, I'm in charge," he told her, "and the four of us

are going to settle this right now. Tim and Ralph are on their way here now, and when we're through, the three of you are going to be acting like you're on a team. Do I make myself clear?"

Ruth nodded, but she was angry. She knew she didn't like Sal Surino, and she wasn't sure that she liked Tommy Francona. Mainly, she wished she didn't have to face Tim Bender and Ralph Madden.

4

When Tim Bender and Ralph Madden entered Tommy's office, they seemed surprised to see Ruth. They also seemed friendly, so she guessed they hadn't seen the newspaper article or even heard about it.

"I'm glad to see that all three of you do more talking than reading," Tommy said sarcastically and gestured for Tim and Ralph to be seated.

"I haven't been talking about a thing," Tim protested.

"Neither have I," Ralph added. "I thought this was all settled."

"We forgot to tell Ruth," Tommy said, handing the paper to Ralph. "Take a look at the second paragraph of Surino's column and then let Tim see it."

The whole thing was embarrassing to Ruth and she stared at the floor while her teammates read Sal Surino's "Sideline Secrets." When they'd finished, the paper was passed back to the Dodger manager. "Well?" Tommy said, waiting for a comment.

"Well, I guess Ruth had a good reason to be mad at us," Ralph said, "but as far as I'm concerned, that's over.

I'm going to let my arm do my talking for the rest of this season."

Tim held out his hand to Ruth. "My daughter jumped all over me for my stupid talk," he told Ruth, shaking her hand, "and by the way, she's playing second on some Little League team. Anyway, I figure we have a pennant to win."

"So do I," Ruth said, smiling warmly, "and I'm all for starting now as if nothing was said by anybody, especially me."

"Done," Tommy said, slamming the newspaper on the desk. "Now get out of here—all of you. I'm not running a school for baby boys or girls, so keep your mouths closed if you can. If you want to say something nice about your manager, that'll be all right, but don't make it too nice. I have a reputation to protect."

Outside Tommy's office, Tim said, "I hear you're starting on Friday."

"I'm supposed to," Ruth said, "but I guess you never know for sure until the first inning."

"You just make sure you're ready," Tim told her. "Ralph and I will be ready whenever we're told that we're starting. Won't we, Ralph?"

"That's right," Ralph agreed, "and if we beat you out in the regular starting rotation, we don't want to hear any excuses about your not being ready. We want to pitch, but when you pitch, we want to see you win. We're all on the same team."

"I know," Ruth said, "and I'll be rooting for you guys whenever you're out there."

As they walked down the ramp to the playing field,

Ruth considered mentioning her little run-in with Maury Jenkins. She felt as if Tim and Ralph would be on her side, but something deep down told her to keep the problem with Maury to herself. It hadn't been a big thing and maybe it was over.

That afternoon, she and Ernie Kirk again reviewed the Angels' batting order. "You know it," Ernie told her, looking pleased, "so just make sure you don't go out partying tonight and forget everything."

"I'm not much for partying," Ruth said.

"Not yet," Ernie said, "but this is a partying town, so don't be surprised if some movie stars and other big shots start inviting you to their get-togethers. You're something of a celebrity, kid. Most of us older guys have seen a few parties in our time. They're fun and the people are all right, as long as you don't take them seriously."

"What's that mean?" Ruth asked.

"It means they want stars, not friends," Ernie told her, "but for now, you just keep your mind on the Angels."

Later, Charley McGraw stopped Ruth and said, "Ernie tells me you're all set for the game tomorrow. What are you doing tonight?"

"I was thinking about some partying," Ruth answered, quickly grinning to assure Charley that she was kidding. "Actually, I don't have anything special planned. Why?"

"Sally and I thought you might want to stop over at our place for an early dinner right after practice," he said. "Sally's anxious to see you, and I'm anxious to see if you've put any dents in my car."

"Your car's okay," Ruth said. "As for dinner, I'd love it.

I've been wanting to see Sally, but I'll have to call Karen and tell her I won't be home for dinner tonight."

"You do that," Charley said, "and I'll see you out in the parking lot. You can follow me."

Driving to the McGraw condominium, Ruth thought about Sally. It would be good to see her again. Back when Ruth was in secret training at the McGraw place in South Carolina, Sally had been like a sister to Ruth. She had made it easier for Ruth to survive the rough training schedule set by Charley. She'd learned a lot from him, but she learned a lot from Sally, too. Mainly, Sally had helped her to see that, despite his gruff manner, Charley really wanted her to be successful.

As soon as Charley pushed open the front door, Sally rushed over to Ruth and hugged her. "Ruth," she said, "you look wonderful. Charley was grumbling about your weight, but you look great to me."

Hugging her back, Ruth laughed. "Charley ran the weight off me. He can be mean, you know."

"Don't I know it," Sally said. "How are your mother and Mike?"

"I talked to Mike last night. He's fine, and my mother's fine, too. She asked about you when I was home."

"Good," Sally answered, "you go on into the living room or wash up if you want. I have to tend to something in the kitchen."

"Come on," Charley said, "I'll show you around the place."

Ruth liked the condo. It was a little bigger than the apartment that Ruth and Karen shared, and the balcony view of the skyscrapers of downtown LA was spectacular.

35

"I still miss South Carolina," Charley told her, "but this'll do for a while."

"I guess so," Ruth said admiringly, just as Sally called her and Charley for dinner.

The food reminded Ruth of her days of living with the McGraws. "Go easy on the biscuits," Charley kidded Ruth. "I wouldn't want to have to make you run around the stadium in Anaheim before the game tomorrow night."

Ruth ate all she wanted. She'd burn off the calories against the Angels. She was sure of that.

During dinner, Charley asked her a little about the Surino column in the *Examiner*. He'd heard most of the story from the Dodger manager, but he was curious as to why Ruth had talked to the columnist. Her explanation made him laugh. "I guess you learned a lesson," he said.

Once again, Ruth thought of her run-in with Maury Jenkins, and once again, she decided to keep the matter to herself. She knew that Charley would help if he could, but it didn't seem right to expect him to fight her battles.

The three of them rested and talked for a little time after dinner, but Charley seemed anxious to send Ruth on her way. "I think you should get a good night's sleep," he told her. "You have a big day ahead of you."

Sally winked at Ruth. "The coach usually knows best," she said.

"Thanks," Charley laughed. "Now don't forget you have to be at the stadium by three tomorrow to catch the team bus, Ruth. If you miss the bus. . ."

"I know," Ruth interrupted, "if I miss the bus, I have to drive to Anaheim and it's a long, tiring drive before a game. I won't miss the bus."

At the door, Sally kissed Ruth on the cheek. "Good luck tomorrow," she said. "I'll be here cheering for you."

"Thanks," Ruth said, "thanks for everything. One of these days, I'll cook and invite the both of you over."

Ruth switched on the car radio during the drive home and tuned in to a sports talk show. People calling into the show made comments and asked questions about the major sports being played in the LA area. One caller sounded off about Ruth. "Sure she pitched well in Albuquerque," he said, "but I don't think she'll be too hot in the majors."

"Why not?" the show's narrator asked.

"Look at the other sports in which women compete," the caller said. "They aren't close to men's records in track, they can't play basketball against the men, and they aren't even strong enough to compete in tennis."

"There's no sense in looking at other sports," the narrator commented. "So far, Ruth Marini is doing fine in baseball. If she isn't some kind of freak, I imagine you'll soon begin to see other women in professional baseball."

"Maybe she is some kind of freak," the caller said. "We'll see."

"I'm sure we will," the narrator said, "and thanks for your call."

Ruth switched off the radio and pulled into her parking space. Her blood was boiling. As far as she was concerned, the caller had been a freak and the show's narrator wasn't much better. She tried to tell herself that she had more important things to think about than two jerks on the radio. Still the talk bothered her.

Karen was out. She'd left a note saying that she had gone out with some friends and wouldn't be home until late. Ruth decided to follow Charley's advice and get to bed. Even though the game the next evening was an exhibition game, she knew it was her first real big league test and she wanted to be ready for it. For a while, she thought about the caller to the radio show. Then she pushed him out of her mind. She fell asleep going over the Angels' batting order in her mind.

5

Ruth lounged around the apartment for most of the next morning. She awakened early enough to talk with Karen before she left for school, but Ruth wasn't in any rush to get dressed. For one thing, she wanted to read what the *Times* had to say about the Dodger-Angel game.

Ruth was pleased with what she read. The story about the game seemed to be straight news. It named the expected starting pitchers and noted that the game marked Ruth's first California start in a Dodger uniform. It also noted that her first regular season game, if and when it was played, would mark the first appearance of a woman in a regularly scheduled major league game. Though Ruth searched, she could find nothing else about the game on the sports pages. She was halfway disappointed, but she realized that stories about her had filled the pages for weeks after she had been named to the team in spring training.

It was near noon when Ruth showered and dressed. Then she searched the refrigerator and settled on a bacon, lettuce, and tomato sandwich for lunch. She was hungrier than that, but she guessed an empty stomach would be best for the game.

An hour later, she made herself another sandwich. There's still a lot of time until the game, she reasoned, so there's no sense in being half-starved by game time. She knew part of the funny feeling in her stomach had nothing to do with being hungry. She was getting anxious about the game, but the extra sandwich seemed to help.

When Ruth climbed onto the team bus, she found it only part full. Some Dodgers lived near the Anaheim Stadium and they'd decided to drive to it. Ruth settled in a seat next to Patch Hasinbiller. Like Ruth, Patch was in his first year with the Dodgers. He'd played Class A ball last year with Lodi of the California League, but he'd hit so well that the Dodgers gave him a trial in spring training. So far, he'd stayed with the team. "How have you been doing?" Ruth asked Patch, who was about her age.

"Pretty good," he replied. "I'm not sure they'll keep me up here, but at the worst, I'll probably end up in Albuquerque. How'd you like it there?"

"Oh, I liked it," Ruth answered, "but I like this better, of course."

"Are you nervous?" Patch asked.

"Why, does it show?"

"No," Patch said, grinning at her, "but I'm nervous and I probably won't even get in the game. I heard the stadium is going to be packed."

"Let's not talk about that," Ruth said. "I'm trying to appear calm."

Patch laughed out loud. "Well, you're sure making me

feel a lot better," he said. "I was beginning to think there was something wrong with me."

"I doubt it," Ruth laughed. "You seem normal to me."

Loud voices from the back of the bus interrupted their conversation. Some of the players were playing cards. "Hey," Tommy Francona yelled from the front of the bus, "if you guys can't play without cheating, I'm going to have to ban the card games. Some of us are trying to get some sleep."

"That's a good idea," Ruth told Patch. "I think I'll try for a short nap."

"Go ahead," Patch said. "I'd do the same if I were pitching tonight."

When the bus slowed for the entrance into Anaheim Stadium, Ruth woke up. "That was fast," she said.

Patch was looking out the bus window at the stadium. "It isn't as big as Dodger Stadium," he said, "but it's gigantic compared to Lodi."

Ruth nodded in agreement, but her mind was racing through the Angels' batting order and her stomach was getting tight. This, she thought, is a big test, even if it's only an exhibition game.

Charley had been sitting in front of the bus, but he was waiting for Ruth as she stepped off. "Let's find out about your dressing facilities," he said.

Ruth followed after him. In his own way, Charley was trying to protect her. He didn't want her getting rattled by some possible problem about dressing, but there wasn't any problem. They were directed to a dressing room with a "Welcome, Ruth Marini" sign on it. "That's nice," Ruth said.

"Yes, it is," Charley agreed. "I'll see you on the field."

Ruth dressed quickly. Her Dodger road uniform fit perfectly, and for a few seconds, she admired her reflection in the mirror. Being a Dodger meant a lot to her. As she stepped out into the tunnel that led to the playing field, she opened and closed her pitching hand. "Don't fail me," she whispered.

"Go out to the bullpen area and warm up with Jerry Parker," Charley told her.

Jerry Parker had played in the big leagues for St. Louis, and after that, he'd joined the Dodgers as a warm-up catcher. He was a stocky, friendly man and Ruth liked working with him.

As Ruth took her warm-up pitches, the expected crowd began to fill the stadium seats.

"Hey, girl," a teenage boy called from the bleachers, "don't get any lipstick on the ball."

Some other kids laughed and Ruth smiled at Jerry. She remembered hearing the same remark back in her high school pitching days.

Other kids called to Ruth and waved papers and books at her for an autograph. She noticed that some girls were wearing baseball caps with "Ruth Marini Fan" printed on them. She wondered how much they cost, but at the same time, she felt happy to see the girls supporting her. A few boys were wearing the caps, too.

"Don't overdo it," Charley said, coming up behind her.

"I'm not," Ruth replied, and Jerry trotted up to join her and Charley.

"It looks as if Ruth has a few fans," Jerry remarked.

"Yeah," Charley agreed, "the cap people are making

some money on her. Listen, Ruth, you take a little break now. Sign a few autographs if you want. You don't have to, but it doesn't hurt to be nice to the kids."

Ruth was happy to hear the suggestion. She'd been wanting to answer the pleas of the kids. She turned and walked over to the seating area.

As Ruth signed the scorecards, sheets of paper, and autograph books, a few wise remarks were hurled at her.

"Sign my bra," a girl called.

"Hey, Ruthie," one boy yelled, "how about a kiss?"

"Go back to New Jersey," a man called. "You don't belong in baseball, Marini."

Ruth had expected the remarks, but many of the kids were surprised by them. "Don't pay any attention to those jerks," a girl told Ruth.

"The Angels' fans are punks," a boy informed her.

"Can I have your phone number?" another boy asked Ruth.

Ruth saw that he was serious. "No, I'm sorry," she said. "I can't do that."

"That's all right," answered the boy, who was about nine years old. "I didn't think you'd give it to me."

Ruth enjoyed being around the kids, but she was happy when Jerry came to her rescue. She quickly signed the bill of a baseball cap being waved at her by a small girl and told the other kids that she had to warm up. They were disappointed, but they surprised her with a cheer as she and Jerry walked off. "You'd better toss a few more," Jerry told her. "It's getting close to game time."

Now Ruth put more effort into her warm-up pitches. Her fastball slammed into Jerry's glove, and her curve

43

broke the way she wanted it to. She was sweating slightly when Jerry pointed to the Dodger dugout. "Time to go," he said, and Ruth climbed into the small electric car for the ride to the playing field.

"I hope you win," the driver said, smiling over at Ruth, "but don't tell anybody on the Angels that I said that."

"Thanks," Ruth replied. "I'll keep it secret."

During the pre-game ceremonies, Charley moved alongside Ruth and said, "Nothing bothering you, is there?"

"I just wish we'd get started," Ruth replied, prompting Charley to pat her on the shoulder.

With the call of "play ball," Ruth and the other Dodgers settled in their dugout seats and yelled encouraging words to the batters. Walt Sawyer was pitching for the Angels, and Ruth watched intently as he set down the Dodgers in order. She quickly slipped off her warm-up jacket and joined the other Dodgers in the run onto the field.

As she smoothed out the mound area to match her pitching stride, Ernie Kirk walked halfway out to her before tossing the ball. "Take all your warm-ups," he said.

The crowd was buzzing with excitement and a ripple of cheers followed after each of Ruth's warm-up pitches. After her last one, Ernie whipped the ball to Luis Santiago on second base, and the plate umpire motioned the first Angel batter to step up to the plate. It was Rick Cole, the first baseman, and the local fans gave him enthusiastic applause. The Dodgers' third baseman tossed the ball to Ruth, and she rubbed it slightly as she looked in for her first signal from Ernie.

Ruth's first pitch cut the inside corner for a called strike. Behind her, she heard the chatter of the infielders. "Way to go," Luis called.

Ruth worked the count to three and two and then really fooled Cole with a changeup. He grinned at her before taking the walk back to his dugout, and Ruth guessed he wouldn't be fooled as easily next time. Still she felt good, and the Dodger fans in the crowd cheered her strikeout pitching.

The next batter was swinging at her first pitch and looped a lazy single into short center field. The throw came into second and Ruth moved into the backup spot. Tossing the ball to her, Luis said, "Get two now."

A bunt by the Angels' third batter caught Ruth and the rest of the Dodgers completely off guard. Ruth managed to get off the mound to field it, but her throw to first was late and the Angels had two runners on base. Walking back to the mound, Ruth glanced at Ralph Jackman getting ready to step into the batter's box. The Angels' fans roared their approval of him. Ruth was amazed by his size. He was bigger than she had imagined and he didn't appear to have an ounce of fat on his body.

Ernie trotted out to the mound, and the crowd booed, suspecting he was going to tell Ruth to walk Jackman. "They must be afraid of you," Ernie said, handing her the ball.

"What makes you think that?" Ruth asked.

"They shouldn't be bunting this early in the game, but they probably figure it's going to be hard to score off you."

45

"They were probably seeing if I know how to field," Ruth replied, "and I guess I didn't show them much."

"Forget it," Ernie suggested. "Let's just get Jackman and the next guy."

"Let's play," the plate umpire called to Ernie.

"Not too fast," Ernie reminded Ruth, as he headed back to his position behind the plate.

Ruth could feel a churning sensation in her stomach. The Angels' fans were chanting "Ralphie, Ralphie," and the runner on first base was taking a huge lead. Ruth brushed the perspiration from her forehead. This is no time to get scared, she told herself, but the feeling was too strong to be ignored.

6

Jackman let Ruth's first pitch go by for a ball. The umpire's call surprised Ruth and Ernie. Holding the ball, Ernie said something to the umpire, who just smiled and dusted off the plate. Ernie took a few steps toward the mound and tossed the ball to Ruth. "Bad call," Ernie said and Ruth made a face to indicate her agreement.

Ruth's next pitch hit the outside corner for a strike, and this time, Jackman didn't like the call. He thumped his bat on the plate and looked menacingly in Ruth's direction. His look had a strange effect on her. Instead of adding to her fear, it calmed her a little. He doesn't scare me, she thought, and reached for the rosin bag.

Jackman was swinging on the next pitch, but he missed with a cut that showed he was going for the fences. "That's pitching," the Dodger shortstop called, and the other infielders joined in the chatter.

On Ruth's next pitch, Jackman was swinging again. His bat made solid contact, but the ball went on a line right to the Dodger left fielder, who gathered it in for out number two.

Once more, Ruth wiped the perspiration from her forehead. One more to go, she thought, and the next batter took care of the thought with a soft grounder to the first baseman, who ran over to the bag and made the out unassisted. As Ruth walked from the mound, two Dodger infielders ran by and each one slapped her on the back. The crowd cheered, and in appreciation, Ruth touched the bill of her cap.

In the top of the third, Goose Gandler, the Dodgers' right fielder, homered with a runner on base, and when Ruth walked to the mound for the bottom of the inning, the scoreboard read, Dodgers 2, Angels 0.

Helped by some great fielding plays, Ruth managed to shut out the Angels until the seventh inning. In the meantime, the Dodgers added two runs to their scoring effort.

Batting for the third time in the seventh, Ralph Jackman got hold of one of Ruth's pitches and drilled it into the right field seats for a home run, making the score 4-1 in favor of the Dodgers. Watching Jackman circle the bases and listening to the wild applause of his fans, Ruth didn't feel too bad. He'd hit home runs off most of the great pitchers during the past decade. She did feel good to think that she wouldn't have to pitch to him during the regular season. He was really powerful.

When Ruth reached the bench at the end of the inning, Charley helped her with her warm-up jacket. "Ralph really tagged you," he said. "Are you getting tired?"

"No," Ruth answered, "the pitch was all right, but he's some hitter."

Charley laughed. "Now you know for sure," he said.

"You don't have to take anybody else's word for that."

In the bottom of the ninth, Ruth sensed that she was tiring. Her fastball wasn't hopping, and her curve was hanging a little. Keep the ball down, she told herself, and then managed to get three Angels to hit into infield outs. After the last out, her infielders gathered around and offered congratulations, and the fans gave her a standing ovation. There were a few boos, but they were drowned out by applause.

"Good game, kid," Tommy said, coming out of the dugout and greeting her.

"Thanks," she said, feeling a big hand on her shoulder.

She turned and saw Ralph Jackman looking down at her. "You pitched fine, Ms. Marini," he told her. "I think you'll make it with the Dodgers."

"Thank you very much," Ruth said, trying to keep from blushing, "but I wish you'd call me 'Ruth,' Mr. Jackman. Getting past you was my hardest job. By the way, you hit a bad pitch out of here."

"I didn't think you were going to give me any good ones, Ruth," he said, winking at her. "Well, anyway, good luck to you."

Ruth shook his hand and thanked him. "Nice hit, Ralph," Charley called, as Jackman walked off toward his own dugout.

"He's a nice guy," Ruth said.

"You wouldn't be saying that if the bases had been loaded when he thumped you," Charley answered. "Now go get showered."

Ruth hustled off toward her dressing room. She was anxious to get out of her perspiration-soaked uniform, but a cry of "wait" stopped her at the dressing room door. It was Tommy Francona. Ruth wondered what the Dodger manager wanted.

"Listen, kid," he said, "a buddy of mine named Sid Mahon from Channel 4 wants to get a couple of minutes from you and me for the late news. Come on, let's talk to him. You'll like Sid. He's a nice guy."

Ruth hesitated. "Will I have time to shower?" she asked.

"Yeah," Tommy said, "after the interview. Don't worry. I'll hold the bus."

Ruth followed Tommy back out onto the playing field. Except for a few stragglers, the stands were empty. Near home plate, Ruth saw a well-dressed man about Tommy's age waving to them. He was holding a mike and two men were standing off to the side. One was holding lighting equipment and the other was holding a TV mini-cam. "Ruth," the well-dressed man said, extending his hand, "I'm Sid Mahon. Thanks, Tommy. I owe you one."

Tommy laughed. "You owe me six," he said, "but let's go. Ruth and I have a bus to catch."

"Let's roll, guys," Sid told his crew, and then turned to Ruth. "You pitched a fine game. I think you're up here to stay."

"Thanks," Ruth replied, just as the lights went on, causing her to blink.

"Let your eyes adjust," Sid said, touching her arm. "I'll talk to Tommy first."

Sid turned to Tommy and the cameraman called, "We're rolling."

"We're lucky tonight, baseball fans," Sid said, smiling

into the camera. "We have the Dodger manager right here, and he is jubilant. Isn't that right, Tommy?"

"Wouldn't you be?" Tommy responded, almost like an actor. "I don't want to put any pressure on Marini, but I think she might be a 20-game winner this year."

"Wait a minute," Sid said. "You're really putting pressure on her."

"Don't worry about it," Tommy said. "She's not afraid of pressure. Go ahead and tell him, Ruth."

Sid turned to her. "Here's Ruth Marini," he said, "and, Ruth, I want to tell you that you pitched a great game tonight. Now what do you think about Tommy's prediction?"

Tommy's prediction was the last thing Ruth wanted to think about. What was really on her mind was how bad she probably looked and how long she was going to be in front of the camera. "I can't think about it," she finally said. "I have to pitch one game at a time. I'm just glad I won tonight."

"Said like a true pro," Sid told the camera. "Well, that's it, folks. Tommy and Ruth have to change and catch the bus back to LA. When we come back, I'll have some other exhibition game scores for you."

The lights went out and Ruth readjusted her sight once more. "Thanks a lot, kid," Sid said to her. "You did fine."

"That's all?" Ruth mumbled.

"Yeah," Tommy said, winking at her. "That's the way Sid is. He gives most of his time to the Angels."

"Go on," Sid said, laughing. "I help to fill that stadium of yours."

"Thanks," Ruth said, heading for the dressing room.

"Thank you," Sid called and then returned to joking with Tommy.

The other players were aboard the bus when Ruth finally climbed up the steps. As she walked up the aisle, her teammates congratulated her, and she in turn congratulated some of them on fielding plays or hits. The only stone face on the bus belonged to Maury Jenkins. He was sitting alone and didn't even bother to nod at Ruth as she passed. After slapping hands with Patch, she settled in the seat next to him. "Where were you?" he asked.

Ruth explained about the interview and a knowing grin spread across Patch's face.

"What's the joke?" Ruth asked.

"No joke," Patch whispered. "It's just that Sid Mahon and Tommy are big buddies. I caught a lot of Sid's interviews on TV last year and you'd be surprised how many times Tommy was on. They almost have a routine."

Ruth laughed. "You know, I noticed that," she said.

"I heard some of the regulars joking about it in the locker room one afternoon," Patch continued whispering, "but I'm not about to make any jokes. I don't want to go back to Lodi if I can help it."

"You're probably misjudging Tommy," Ruth said. "He seems like a goodhearted guy."

"Yeah," Patch agreed, "but I'll be a little less nervous after my first 20 home runs."

"I can't wait," Ruth said, hoping to encourage him.

A few minutes later, the Dodger manager entered the bus and it set off for their home grounds. The air conditioning made Ruth drowsy and the next thing she knew, Patch was gently squeezing her shoulder. "We're home," he said.

Tommy was standing in the aisle and motioning for quiet. "In case any of you have forgotten, we play the Angels here tomorrow night. Be here by four. Jenkins is our starter."

Tommy's last sentence surprised Ruth. She didn't think Maury Jenkins had looked too good in practice. She wondered if the decision to use him was something suggested by Charley. A few players called "good luck" to Maury, but if he was happy about the opportunity, he was keeping it to himself. "Not a friendly guy," Patch whispered.

"That's true," Ruth whispered back, feeling somewhat relieved to know she wasn't alone.

During the drive home Ruth turned her radio dial to the sports talk show. Not one caller mentioned her, and she realized she was disappointed. She guessed she would have had some mention if she had lost and her disappointment quickly faded.

Karen greeted Ruth at the door and praised her winning effort. "I watched the whole game," she said, "and you should have heard the announcer raving about you. He said he thought you were the best Dodger rookie pitcher since Fernando."

"I wish I were that good," Ruth answered.

"Oh, by the way, you just missed Mike," Karen said.

"Mike who?"

Karen smiled. "Mike Garcia, your man. He called a little while ago. He'd heard the score on the late news in New Jersey and wanted to congratulate you."

53

"Did he say to call back?" Ruth asked, glancing at the clock on the kitchen wall.

"No," Karen replied, "he said it was late there and he had to get to bed. I think he had a lot to do in the morning. You know, he really sounds like a great guy. He told me that he might come out here sometime this summer."

"He did?" Ruth said. "That's news to me."

"Oh, stupid me. Maybe he was going to surprise you."

"I guess so," Ruth answered, still startled by the news. "I'll call him tomorrow, but I won't let on about his visit."

"Good," Karen said. "I wouldn't want him to think I was a jerk."

Later, Ruth found it difficult to fall asleep. She was anxious to know if Mike was really coming to LA, but something else was bothering her, too. She felt some small pangs of jealousy about Mike's conversation with Karen. It sounded as if they had become very friendly. Back in Union City, Ruth had spent a lot of time telling Mike how much he would like Karen if he met her. He hadn't really met her yet, but it sounded as if he liked her all right. Ruth tried to tell herself she was thinking like a high school girl, but this did seem different. Karen was bright and beautiful, and Mike. . .

"This is crazy," Ruth finally decided, and she began to think about something really important—her pitching performance. Minutes later, she was fast asleep.

7

Ruth was frustrated when she left for Dodger Stadium the next afternoon. No one had answered her several calls to Mike's home, and she couldn't imagine where the Garcia family might be. She was anxious to speak with Mike or, at least, leave a message for him to call.

Before leaving for school, Karen had aroused Ruth's jealousy again by asking to see a picture of Mike. "He's as good looking as he sounds," she had told Ruth, and Ruth had had to bite her lip to hold back a nasty response.

Despite her frustration, Ruth was pleased by a glowing report of her victory over the Angels in the *Times*' sports section. She had, according to the reporter, performed like a seasoned veteran rather than a young rookie. Alongside the story was a picture of Ruth signing autographs. She couldn't recall seeing the photographer, but she felt proud of the picture and wondered if it would appear in the New Jersey papers. If it did, she knew her mother would cut it out and place it in the scrapbook she was keeping.

That evening, Ruth found herself rooting for Maury

Jenkins. He pitched well enough to win on most evenings, but the Dodgers couldn't string even two hits back to back against the Angels' starting pitcher. Maury suffered a tough 1-0 loss, and the exhibition series between the Dodgers and their local rival was tied at one win apiece.

Later that night, Ruth tried again to reach Mike. He wasn't home, but his father answered the phone. Although he sounded friendly, Ruth guessed that she had awakened him with her late call. "Just tell Mike I called, please," she said, before putting down the receiver.

Over breakfast the next morning, Karen talked on and on about some super guy in one of her classes, and Ruth realized how foolish her jealousy had been. She had been thinking like a high school girl. Despite all that had happened to her in the last few years, she still had a lot of growing up to do. Listening to Karen's eager chatter, Ruth hoped she could learn to be a better friend.

The Dodgers played the Angels again that evening, and a huge crowd filled Dodger Stadium for what would be the final exhibition game for both teams. Tim Bender started for the Dodgers, but both teams went on a hitting spree, and by the fifth inning, neither starting pitcher had survived.

With one out in the bottom of the ninth and the score tied at 6-6, Goose Gandler drilled a line drive into the right field corner. Playing the hit off the wall, the Angels' outfielder bobbled the ball a couple of times before making the long throw to third. Goose slid in under the tag with a triple, and the cheering of the Dodger fans rocked the stadium.

Ruth joined in the applause and chatter of the moment,

but she quickly turned her attention to home plate when she heard the public address announcer say, "Batting for the Dodgers, number 72, Patch Hasinbiller."

Come on, Patch, Ruth mumbled to herself. She didn't envy him. The Dodger fans sounded as if they were at the seventh game of a World Series rather than a preseason exhibition game. They wanted a hit.

Patch attempted a bunt on the first pitch, but it went foul. Some of the fans booed. Ruth wasn't sure if they were booing the bunt or Tommy's decision to call for a bunt. Ruth looked down toward the other end of the dugout. The Dodger manager seemed tense. Maybe he was having second thoughts about sending Patch up there.

After taking a ball, Patch attempted another bunt and this one went up in the air behind the plate. The Angels' catcher got his glove on the ball, but it bounced out into the dirt for strike two. Ruth let out some air. Patch had been lucky on that one. Now he'd be hitting. A foul bunt on a third strike play would be ruled a strikeout, and the Dodgers couldn't risk that with the score tied. Ruth watched as Patch stepped out of the box and took a few practice swings. Except for some buzzing, the crowd had become silent as Patch stepped back into the box and Goose took a short lead off third.

Ruth held her breath as the Angel pitcher got set for his delivery. The ball moved toward the plate, and Patch swung at it and connected. He lifted a fly ball to center, and the Angel outfielder moved in for the catch as Goose hustled back to third. A groan of disappointment issued from the crowd and Ruth felt the same way. It looked like an easy out. Hoping for an error, Ruth watched the ball drop into the gloved hand of the Angel outfielder for out number two. But the play wasn't over. Goose had tagged up and was making a run for the plate. He wasn't the speediest Dodger player, but his move had caught the Angels off guard. The outfielder whipped the ball toward the plate, and Goose arrived there about the same time. The play was close, and for a second, the plate umpire hesitated. Then he gave the flat palm signal.

The crowd in Dodger Stadium went wild. Goose had scored. The game was over and the Dodgers had won 7-6. The players rushed out onto the field to congratulate Goose. Ruth rushed out too, but she ran to Patch. "Good hit," she said, hugging him. "You batted in the winning run."

"Yeah," Patch said, cheered by her praise, "I guess I did."

"Good work, kid," the Dodger manager called to Patch.

"Thanks," Patch called back. Then he turned to Ruth. "Say, where are you going after you change?"

"Home."

"A couple of the other guys and I are going over to a place on Vermont called Luigi's," Patch said. "We'll have some pizzas and watch the show. They have singing waiters and waitresses. Want to join us? I'm buying. It'll be a mini-celebration of your game and my sacrifice fly."

The thought of calling Mike flashed through Ruth's mind, but the call could wait. It wasn't an emergency. "Sure, I'll go," Ruth said, "How about some directions?"

Rather than worry about fouling up the directions, Patch suggested that Ruth meet him in the parking lot and follow him to the restaurant.

Luigi's was in the Hollywood section of Vermont Avenue, and as Ruth followed Patch, she was glad to see that she was close to Glendale. She imagined she could find her way home later without any difficulty.

Inside the restaurant, they spotted Jeff Durante, a second-year Dodger who was a substitute infielder, and Ripper Rippard, another second-year player who backed up the regular catcher and pinch hit. "Welcome to our favorite hangout," Jeff said, motioning for them to be seated.

"Hey, this is a nice place," Patch remarked.

"Yes," Ruth agreed, "but haven't you been here before?"

"Them, not me," Patch said. "I was just repeating what they told me. When it comes to LA, I haven't been anywhere before."

"But he's known around Lodi as a swinger," Ripper kidded, winking at Ruth.

"Hey," Patch said, "I grew up in Cleveland. I didn't even know that there were towns as small as Lodi."

Ruth and the others laughed. "I like LA," Jeff said, as a beaming waitress passed out menus. "Most of the people up north think it's the pits, but I've come around to thinking it's a pretty good place to live."

"Up north?" Ruth said, puzzled by the remark.

"San Francisco," Jeff explained. "We call LA down south."

"Boy, this isn't the south," Ripper remarked. "Jackson, Mississippi, was the south and I'm not going back there if I can help it."

"I thought all that color stuff was over down there," Patch said.

Ripper laughed. "Maybe it is," he said, "but that doesn't make Mississippi into heaven, does it? White folks' kids are leaving all the time. I'll take LA. In bad times, I might even settle for Lodi."

They laughed again before Ruth said, "I'm from Union City, New Jersey."

"We all know that," Ripper joked. "Your short life story has been in every magazine and on every TV news show in the world."

Ruth blushed slightly. "Hey, don't embarrass her," Patch said, grinning good-naturedly at Ruth.

"Yeah," Jeff added, "you saw how much she got rattled on the mound the other night."

"You're some sweet pitcher," Ripper said, opening his menu. "Now let's get down to some overeating. How about a large house special to start with?"

Ripper wasn't kidding about overeating. The house special pizza came covered with about 10 toppings. Ruth loved it and so did the others. After they had devoured three of the specials, they ordered some coffee. While they'd been eating, their waitress had stepped onto the restaurant's small stage and sung a few songs. She had a good voice, and Jeff explained that she and the other waitresses and waiters often appeared in shows in the LA area. Ruth wasn't positive, but she guessed their waitress and Jeff had an interest in one another.

After coffee, Ruth pulled out her wallet. "Put that away," Patch said. "I told you this was going to be on me."

"Mine, too?" Ripper joked.

Ruth didn't argue. "Well, thanks," she said. "Now if

you guys don't mind, I'm going home."

"I'll walk you out to your car," Patch said, throwing some money onto the table. "I'll see you guys in a minute."

"You'd better," Jeff said as he counted Patch's money. "This isn't going to cover the coffee and the big tip for our lovely waitress."

Patch followed Ruth out to the parking lot behind Luigi's. "Well, I hope you had a good time," he said.

"The best time I've had since I got here," Ruth answered.

"Listen," Patch said as she inserted her key in the door lock, "what do you think about going out with guys on your team?"

Patch's question caught Ruth completely off guard. She didn't know if he was speaking about himself. "I never gave it a thought," she confessed.

"Well, you think about it," Patch said, "and remember, I may not be on your team all year."

Smiling slightly, Ruth touched his arm and said, "Did you practice that last line?"

"Not enough," Patch replied, laughing at himself. "I'll see you on Monday."

Ruth climbed into her car. As she pulled away, Patch waved at her. She halfway wished that she'd had the nerve to say "yes" to his question. They could be friends. It was not such a big deal. By the time she reached home, she was thinking about Mike again.

8

"Phone call," Karen said, shaking Ruth out of the long sleep she had planned for Saturday morning. "It's Mike."

Groggy but pleased, Ruth reached for the extension phone next to her bed, and Karen returned to the kitchen to hang up the receiver there. "Sorry to wake you," Mike said, "but I wanted to catch you before practice."

"No practice until Monday," Ruth explained. "Thursday is opening day."

"I know," Mike said, "and the *Dispatch* is predicting that you'll be the Dodger starter. By the way, that was a great game you pitched the other night."

"Thanks, but don't believe everything you read in the *Dispatch*. The opening day starter hasn't been named and I'd be surprised if I get the assignment. We have a lot of good pitchers."

"Well, you're my pick," Mike replied. "So how have you been?"

"Fine," Ruth said. "My apartment's real nice and Karen has been great."

"I talked with her the other night. She sounds nice. By

the way, I don't know if she told you, but I may be able to get out there sometime in August."

"You will?" Ruth answered, trying to sound surprised. "How'd you swing it?"

"We're finishing up one job around August 1, and another one isn't scheduled until mid-August. So I figured seeing you might be a good way to spend my hard-earned money."

"Right," Ruth said cheerfully. "I'll be counting the days."

They talked on, exchanging a little gossip about Union City and the Dodgers. Ruth wanted to ask Mike if he had been seeing anyone else, but common sense steered her away from that question and away from mentioning her new friendship with Patch. Finally and reluctantly, they hung up.

Ruth rolled over and tried for some more sleep, but the ringing of the phone woke her again. This time it was Sally McGraw. "How would you like to go shopping with me this afternoon?" she asked. "I'm driving over to Beverly Hills. I may not buy anything, but we can look."

The idea excited Ruth. She was eager to get together with Sally, and she also wanted to see the place where the rich people of Southern California spent their money. Instead of leaving in the afternoon, they decided to get together earlier and have lunch in Beverly Hills.

They ate in Nate 'n Al's, a deli-style restaurant that, according to Sally, was a regular hangout of many Hollywood stars. Aside from the pictures on the walls, Ruth didn't see any stars, but she learned that she was becoming one. Several people came over to their table and asked Ruth for her autograph. Ruth signed the sheets of paper, but she couldn't hide her embarrassment. Sally laughed at her after the autograph hunters left. "You're going to have to get used to fame," she said, "and that reminds me about a strange phone call we received last night. Some guy called and said that he was your father. He wanted your phone number. I figured he was just some jerk, so I hung up on him."

"I'm glad you didn't give him my number," Ruth said. "I'm sure it wasn't my father, and even if it were, I wouldn't want to talk to him. What it sounds like is a rotten joke dreamed up by some sicky."

"You wouldn't even know your father, would you?" Sally asked.

"No," Ruth admitted, "I've seen pictures of him, but they'd have to be at least 20 years old. He just disappeared when I was a baby, but I guess I've told you that."

"You have. I was just wondering if you'd heard anything about him over the years."

"Not a thing," Ruth shrugged. "His brother, my uncle, lived in Pennsylvania and used to visit my mother and me when I was little. He was all right, but even he didn't know anything about my father. I haven't seen that uncle in about eight years. I don't even know if he's alive, though I guess he should be. He isn't real old. We never were close with him. I think he always felt ashamed about his brother. After a while, we lost contact with him. You know how those things are."

"I sure do," Sally said, smearing mustard on her pastrami sandwich. "I have a lot of relatives that I've never seen in my life."

"I don't know why my father left," Ruth went on. "My mother doesn't know either. They didn't have any big fights or anything. He just left for work one day and never came home. For a while, my mother thought he might have been murdered or hurt in an accident, but then someone she knew saw my father on the street in Cliffside Park. That's a city near Union City. He told that person he was making a new life for himself and he didn't bother to ask about me or my mother. That was it. We never heard another word. I guess my mother could have gone to court and tried to find him for support, but she was too proud for that. We got by."

Sally reached across the table and patted Ruth's hand. "You did more than get by," she said. "You're both wonderful people."

"Hey," Ruth said, 'I wasn't looking for sympathy, but if that sicky calls you again, slam down the phone as hard as you can. His ears will be ringing for weeks."

"Okay," Sally answered. "I was beginning to forget that you're a tough ballplayer."

After lunch, they walked through the Beverly Hills shopping area, stopping and going through a few stores along the way. Neither woman purchased a thing. "These prices are outrageous," Ruth told Sally, and all Sally could do was laugh in agreement.

"Well, it was a pleasant way to waste an afternoon," Sally said, as they settled into her car.

"It was fun," Ruth replied, "but I don't think it'll ever be my regular shopping area."

"I hope not. Even if Charley and I were rich, I don't think I'd be able to throw the money away. I guess I'll always be something of a country girl."

"Me, too," Ruth jokingly responded.

During the ride back to Ruth's apartment, Sally extended an invitation for dinner at her place, but Ruth couldn't accept because she'd planned to go to dinner and a movie with Karen.

The dinner turned out to be terrible. She and Karen had picked a new Mexican restaurant in Glendale. It was too new. It seemed as if they had to wait forever for their food and almost as long for their check. Only some speedy driving by Karen kept them from being late for the movie, which was better than they had expected.

After the movie, they returned home. Karen had some schoolwork to catch up on, and Ruth was exhausted. "I'm going to bed," she told Karen while trying to smother a huge yawn. "I got more tired from an afternoon of shopping than I do from a whole day of practice. I'll see you in the morning."

9

The next day when Ruth got to her dressing room in the Dodger stadium, Sam Larkin, the clubhouse manager, handed her an envelope with her name on it.

"Probably a fan letter," he said. "It was addressed in care of the team office."

Ruth looked curiously at the name and address written in ballpoint pen on the crumpled envelope. She didn't have time to read the letter before practice, so she stuffed it into her jacket pocket. When Ruth got back to the apartment that evening, she remembered it.

It wasn't a fan letter. The few lines scrawled on the single sheet of paper had a different kind of message.

> Dear Ruth,
> I've been trying to get in touch with you, and I decided to write. I'm living in LA now and I thought we could get together. Please write me at this address.
> I really want to see you, Ruth.

The letter was signed "Frank Marini."

When Karen came into the living room a few minutes

later, Ruth was sitting with the sheet of paper in her hand and tears running down her face. Hurrying to Ruth's side, Karen asked gently, "What is it?"

Ruth couldn't respond. Instead of Karen's voice, she was hearing a voice from the past, from her childhood. "My daddy's a mailman," one of her young friends was saying. "What is your daddy?"

Her mind jumped to first grade. "Now children," the teacher was saying, "tomorrow we're going to make cards for Father's Day. You all want to make something nice for your daddies, don't you?"

One after another, the painful events of her childhood replayed themselves in her mind's eye. She thought she'd forgotten most of them. Instead, they'd been locked up, and like some sinister magic, the letter had unleashed them. She remembered how some of those events had caused her to cry and seek the comfort of her mother's arms. As she got control of herself, she realized that Karen was holding her and patting her back. "I'm so sorry," Ruth said. "You must think I'm losing my mind."

"No," Karen said soothingly, "you just take your time and calm down. I'm your friend, and I want to help."

Ruth blew her nose and rested. "I'm okay," she finally said, managing to smile weakly at Karen. "This letter brought back some bad memories, but I'm okay now. I mean it."

"Good," Karen said, "I'll make us some coffee and maybe we can talk about it."

While Karen readied the coffee, Ruth washed her face. She was still upset about the letter, but in a sense, she felt good. She'd kept those memories bottled up for a long time, and she was glad they were out. She was probably old enough to handle them now. She was certainly old enough to share them with a friend. "Are you ready for a long story?" she asked Karen.

"I'm listening," her roommate answered.

When Ruth finished, Karen sat quietly with a frown on her face. Finally, she said, "But after all these years, do you think your father would try to get in touch with you? Do you really think that letter is from him?"

"You know," Ruth replied, seeming surprised by her own words, "I think it might be."

"What makes you think that?"

"I don't know," Ruth answered, "but it just seems strange that a guy would write and pretend to be my father. Even if he'd learned that my father ran off when I was little, he couldn't know for sure that I'd never seen or heard from him since. That part doesn't make sense."

"Listen, creeps try anything. The world is filled with weird people who want to get close to celebrities. The guy who shot at the president used to make calls to some TV star. I can't think of her name. And even if it was your father, you don't want to see him, do you?"

"No," Ruth said emphatically, "I don't want to have anything to do with him."

The next evening, a call came for Ruth. It was her mother. "What's been happening, Ruth," she asked.

"A lot," Ruth replied. "I'll tell you, but just let me go through the whole thing before you start asking questions."

When Ruth was finished, her mother said, "Karen is right. It was probably just some sick person. Don't answer the letter and that'll be the end of that."

"Mom," Ruth said questioningly, "do you have any pictures of him?"

"Who?"

"My father. Frank Marini," Ruth said. "I remember you used to have some. We used to look at them when I was little."

"I still have them," her mother said. "I'll send you one, but don't start thinking you're going to meet your father. Even if he was proud to be the father of a big baseball star, he'd have sense enough to know that he hurt you. Frank was never dumb."

"I'm not thinking of meeting anyone," Ruth said, "but if some creep ever walks up to me saying that he's my father, I'd like to be able to call for the cops and not have it come out that the creep really is my father. If it is him, I can just walk away."

"I'll send the picture," Mrs. Marini replied. "Now tell me what else has been happening to you? Are you eating enough?"

After the call, Ruth thought about how much her relationship with her mother had changed in a couple of years. Their love was still strong, but there wasn't much to talk about. They lived in different worlds now and Ruth guessed they'd never be as close as they had been. It probably has more to do with growing up than moving away, she thought.

At practice the next day, Ruth tried to put the letter out of her mind, but that night, she called Sally McGraw and told her about what had happened. Sally had some news for Ruth, too. Maury Jenkins was going to be the Dodger pitcher on opening day. "Charley wanted you,"

Sally said, "but Tommy overruled him. You keep that to yourself. Don't even mention it to Charley."

Ruth couldn't hide her disappointment. "I guess I really wanted it," she told Sally, "and to be honest, I don't like Maury Jenkins."

Sally laughed out loud, "That's all right," she said. "Maury Jenkins doesn't like you or anybody else. He and Charley have come close to slugging it out, but Charley admits that his pitching is good. It's too bad that his personality stinks."

"Yeah," Ruth laughed, "it does."

If Maury Jenkins smiled at all during the opening day game, Ruth missed it. He pitched a good game, though, stopping the Reds with a four-hitter. The Dodgers left the field with a 5-1 victory.

Two nights later, Ruth started her first regular big league game. It was the last of a three-game series with the Cincinnati Reds, who had managed a 7-5 win in the second game.

As usual, Dodger fans filled the stadium, and they cheered wildly when the public address announcer called off Ruth's name and number. The cheering didn't help to settle Ruth's stomach. The nervousness in there wasn't something new to her. She had felt it before other games, and it always went away as soon as the game started. "Go to it, kid," Tommy said, slapping her on the back when the umpire called, "Play ball."

More cheers greeted Ruth as she hustled out to the mound. The cheering died down as she made her warm-up pitches, but when the first Red stepped up to the plate, a surprisingly loud roar of boos issued from the stands. A glance at the Reds' bench explained the booing to Ruth. Several Reds players were waving pink, flower-decorated towels at Ruth. "Your shower's ready, lady," one called.

"Hey, Ruthie," another called, "are you pregnant yet?"

In spite of the warnings she'd had, Ruth really was rattled slightly by the Reds. She turned away and looked in for the signal as the Dodger infield started some chatter behind her.

The plate umpire had called "time out" and was striding over to the Reds' bench. He was going to warn the players to keep the towels inside the dugout so they wouldn't cause a distraction, and the Dodger fans quickly applauded his actions. Ruth threw another warm-up pitch to her catcher. She could feel a little tightness in her shoulder, but she figured it would work its way out once they got started.

Five pitches later, Ruth recorded her first big league strikeout and forgot that there had been any tightness in her shoulder. Her stomach felt better, too. The handful of Reds who were trying to rattle her kept up their remarks, but she resolved not to let them get to her.

When the top of the fifth inning rolled around, the Dodgers were leading 2-0, and the Reds had only managed one hit off Ruth. The first batter in the fifth was the Reds' catcher, and he surprised Ruth with a drag bunt down the first base line. She rushed over to field it, and as she reached down for the rolling ball, she heard the heavy steps of the oncoming batter. He hit her hard, and she felt the ball twist out of her grasp as her body rolled onto the dirt in foul territory. Slightly dazed, Ruth looked up and saw players racing onto the field from both benches.

Fists were flying all around Ruth when she climbed to her feet. It looked like a free-for-all, and for a moment, she was puzzled. She wasn't sure if she should join in or get out of the way. Patch settled the question for her when he grabbed her arm and said, "Are you okay?"

"I guess so," Ruth answered, seeing that the umpires and managers were waving players back to their respective benches.

"Are you all right?" a voice behind her asked. This time, it was Charley, and he was dabbing his handkerchief at some blood running out of his nose.

"I should be asking you," Ruth answered, brushing the dirt from her uniform, "but I'm fine."

"Good," Charley said, looking at his red-stained handkerchief and grinning. "You probably didn't know I was a catcher, did you?"

"Good catch," Ruth laughed.

Aside from Charley, Ruth couldn't see any player who had suffered much damage. She was glad no one had decided to carry a bat into the fray because bats were a lot more dangerous than fists.

The bunt that had started the battle was ruled a hit, but Ruth managed to set down the next three batters. In the bottom half of the inning, her teammates treated her to another three runs, giving the Dodgers a solid 5-0 lead.

Over the next four innings, Ruth concentrated on keeping her pitches low and letting her fielders do the work. In the seventh, the Reds pushed one run across the plate, but aside from that, Ruth experienced little trouble. When the last out was called at first base in the ninth inning, she trotted off the field with her first big league win. The Dodger fans gave her a standing ovation. "You just got yourself a line in the baseball record book," Tommy said, giving her a hearty hug.

Ruth laughed. "I would have gotten that line even if I lost."

"Yeah," Tommy agreed, "but it'll read better this way."

Ruth couldn't argue with that. She saw Patch coming over to congratulate her and surprised herself by saying, "If you're interested in celebrating, I'll buy the pizza tonight."

He was.

10

Four days later, Ruth got her second starting assignment, against the Houston Astros. Before the game a special visitor came to her dressing room. It was Gene Webber, the owner of the Dodgers. "I guess you were wondering if I've been paying any attention to you," he said. "Well, I have and you're doing just fine. Any problems you can't handle?"

"Not so far," Ruth replied, "but I'll probably be a little more careful on bunts tonight."

Mr. Webber laughed. "That was some brawl the other night," he said. "It reminded me of the old days when the Dodgers were in Brooklyn and Durocher was our manager. The runner could have gone around you, but I'm glad to see that our team was right behind you. We had trouble with a few of our players during Jackie Robinson's first year. They claimed they didn't want to play with him. The following year, they were playing against him, but I'm glad we don't have any of that trouble with you."

"So am I," Ruth agreed, beginning to feel anxious about getting out on the field.

"You go on now," Gene Webber told her. "I'll be up in my box rooting for you."

Ruth lasted eight innings that night. In the ninth, she walked the first two batters and Tommy called time out. Judging from the look on his face as he walked to the pitcher's mound, Ruth guessed she was through for the evening. "We're sitting on a 7-2 lead," Tommy told her. "You pitched a good game, but I think you're ready for a little relief."

"You're the boss," Ruth answered, handing him the ball.

As soon as Dilly Bickle, the Dodgers' ace reliever, reached the mound, Ruth headed for the dugout. She was disappointed, but the Dodger fans were obviously satisfied with her performance. They stood and cheered, and Ruth tipped her cap to acknowledge their applause. "Don't look so sad," Charley told her. "Dilly will save the game and you'll walk out of here tonight with a 2-0 record."

"Yeah," Ruth said, not cheered by Charley's logic, "but I don't know why I couldn't hit the strike zone."

"That's easy," Charley said, glancing down at the statistics book that he kept. "You threw about 30 more pitches than you did the other night. You were getting behind on the batters because you were trying too hard for the corners of the zone."

"Why didn't you tell me earlier?" Ruth asked.

Charley grinned at her. "I make it a habit not to interfere in a winning game. Now put on your jacket and watch Dilly. You can learn something from watching him."

Ruth watched, but Dilly wasn't out there long enough for Ruth to learn much. The first batter that he faced fouled out to the Dodger third baseman, and the next batter grounded into a double play on the first pitch thrown to him. Ruth joined the other Dodgers in congratulating Dilly on his save. "It got me another win," she told him.

"My pleasure," he responded.

As Ruth headed for the clubhouse passageway, Maury Jenkins fell in alongside of her. "They're starting to get to you," he remarked with an unpleasant smile on his face.

"You'll be gone before me," she replied, trying to smile back in the same way.

"Oh, yeah," he said. "If you were a man, you'd be picking up your teeth for a remark like that."

Ruth stopped and turned toward him. She could feel her hands closing into fists and her stomach twisting into knots. "Why don't you just make believe that I'm a man?" she said.

"Hey, what's going on here?" Goose Gandler asked as he came up behind them.

"Nothing," Maury answered, "nothing at all."

"Just talk," Ruth said, trying to calm herself.

Goose wasn't fooled. "Talk tomorrow," he said, throwing his huge arm around Maury's shoulder and nodding at Ruth. "They're going to turn the hot water off soon."

Goose steered Maury through the door of their dressing room and Ruth moved up the passageway. For the time being, it was over with Maury, but she was sure it wasn't over for good. While showering, she had to laugh at her

77

response to Maury. She could pitch, but she couldn't fight. She was sure of that.

Late that night, Mike called. Ruth told him all about the letter from the man who said he was her father. She also told him about the picture she had received from her mother. "I really don't want to see my father," she said, "but I have to admit that I look a little like him."

Sensing Ruth's uneasiness about her father, Mike changed the subject. "You pitched a good game tonight. I caught the score on the late news."

"I threw too many pitches," Ruth explained, parroting the information supplied by Charley, "so I needed help in the ninth."

"That's why every team has a staff of relief pitchers," Mike responded. "No pitcher goes the full distance every game."

"Thanks for filling me in," Ruth said kiddingly.

"I'm always willing to help," Mike kidded back.

They talked a while longer, and when Ruth put down the receiver, she realized how much she missed him. She enjoyed being with Patch the couple of times they had gotten together, but Mike was special.

Two days later, the Dodgers journeyed south to San Diego for their first game on the road. While checking into their hotel, several Dodgers kidded Ruth about being assigned to room with her. Ruth didn't mind the teasing. It was the players' way of showing that they liked her. Still she halfway wished that there were another woman on the team.

Ruth gave two interviews while in San Diego. The first was for a local TV show that featured women in the news. Ruth struggled through that interview because the person asking the questions seemed to want Ruth to say that she was being treated poorly. Ruth couldn't blame the interviewer because, as she had learned back in high school English, bad news makes for bigger audiences.

The second interview was for a national news service, and it followed Ruth's third straight victory, a 2-0, three-hit shutout of San Diego. The reporter had been born and raised in Jersey City and knew many people in Union City. For once, Ruth actually enjoyed an interview.

The Dodgers moved on to Atlanta and although she needed relief in the seventh inning, Ruth scored her fourth straight victory there. The fans there treated her well for an opposing pitcher, but an event staged in front of the Dodgers' hotel angered Ruth. A group of women paraded with signs that read: "Keep women out of baseball. Baseball is a man's game."

From what Ruth could gather, the women were afraid their daughters would become interested in playing baseball. How baseball was going to ruin the lives of young women was something Ruth and the people who interviewed the group for an Atlanta television station couldn't find out. "Just forget them," Charley advised Ruth. "They're leftovers from the last century."

Ruth's next appearance on the mound was against the Cincinnati Reds. She expected them to be a lot tougher in their home park. The Reds' fans filled the stadium, and thousands of them came with pink towels to wave at Ruth. They also chanted "bunt" from the bottom of the first inning on.

The towels and chanting didn't bother Ruth, but her

pitching wasn't sharp. Only good fielding by the Dodgers kept the Reds from scoring in the first and second inning. It was a cool night and Ruth thought her control would improve as she warmed up in the later innings.

In the top of the third, Ruth took her turn at bat and looped a soft liner over the head of the Reds' first baseman. She pulled up at first base with a single. It was her first big league hit. "Don't steal," the Reds' first baseman said, joking with her.

"I'll go if they send me," she joked back, knowing well that she'd never get a signal to steal.

When the count on the next Dodger batter reached three balls and two strikes, Ruth did get a signal to run and she took off with the pitch. She was rounding second when the Reds' left fielder drifted in and caught the short fly ball for out number three.

Ruth's control wasn't any sharper in the bottom of the third. After walking the leadoff man, she allowed a single by the next batter and the Red on first scooted all the way to third.

Watching the runners and pitching too carefully, Ruth walked the third batter, loading the bases. As she expected, Tommy called "time" and slowly walked out to the pitcher's mound. "You don't have it tonight, do you?" he said as soon as he reached her.

"They haven't scored yet," she answered defensively.

"That's true," Tommy said, turning to the Dodger catcher. "What do you think?"

"She's off," he answered, "but maybe she's cold."

"Why don't we call it a night?" Tommy said to Ruth.

"Hey," Ruth replied, balking at the suggestion, "they

haven't even scored a run yet."

"I know," Tommy said, almost apologetically, "but I don't like the way you're throwing and I want to make a change."

The plate umpire had walked to the mound. "Let's get going," he said. "The people came to see a ballgame."

"We're bringing in a new pitcher," Tommy told him and held out his hand for the ball.

Ruth slipped the ball into his hand and started off the mound. A mild ripple of applause came from the stands as she headed for the dugout, but for the most part, the fans waved their towels and booed.

"Tough night," Charley said as soon as she stepped into the dugout.

"What's with him?" Ruth asked, motioning toward Tommy.

"You were pitching lousy," Charley responded. "Sure he could have waited until they scored off you. Or do you want to tell me you were in good form?"

"The towels didn't bother me," Ruth remarked, "I was a little off from the start."

Charley laughed. "Go sit down or head for the shower," he said. "No one cares about the towels except the bright guy who thought of selling them."

Ruth stuck around until the end of the inning. The relief pitching was good, but the Reds managed to score one run on a sacrifice fly. The score was 1-0 in favor of the Reds.

After showering, Ruth hung around her dressing room and listened to the rest of the game on the radio. The one run that the Reds had scored turned out to be all they needed because their pitcher shut out the Dodgers on three hits. Because the runner who had scored was Ruth's responsibility, she was tagged with her first loss of the season and her record stood at 4-1.

Three days later, Tommy gave her another shot at win number five, and she whipped the Cardinals 4-2. She also put a quick end to the fans' idea of stopping Ruth Marini with towels. The Cardinal fans had purchased a fair share of them, but they'd stopped waving them around the seventh inning. Patch made a pinch-hit double in the fourth inning and finished the game in the outfield.

That night, Ruth and Patch celebrated with a steak dinner at a St. Louis restaurant near their hotel. Ruth was pleased by Patch's success and she realized her interest in him was growing. It was good to have a close friend on the team. Though Ruth was very fond of Charley, she regarded him more like an older brother.

The following night after a loss to the Cardinals, the Dodgers climbed aboard their plane and headed for home. Their first road trip had been a winning one, but they were sitting in third place two games behind the Giants. In the Eastern Division, the Phillies were leading by three games and they were playing as if they were going to run away with the division title.

Ruth arrived home very late that night and though she didn't expect it, she was delighted to find Karen waiting to greet her. "You have the most wins in the league," Karen said. "You sure must be proud of yourself."

"I guess I am," Ruth replied, "but you didn't stay up just to tell me my pitching record, did you?"

Karen laughed. "Of course not. I stayed up to ask you

about the road trip and find out about all the interesting things that never get in the newspaper."

Curling up on the couch, Ruth smiled at her friend. "I'm glad you waited up for me. I missed being able to talk with you. The guys treat me all right, but I don't really hang around with them, so it gets a little boring on the road."

"Well, tell me all the details. What kind of dressing room facilities did you have?" Karen asked.

"They were pretty good," Ruth answered. "Everybody had something fixed up for me. They're building a new dressing room in Atlanta, but it wasn't quite finished, so I got to use the Atlanta manager's dressing room and he got to shower with his players."

Karen laughed out loud. "I didn't know he was a gentleman," she said. "Say, would a gentleman offer a lady his private shower?"

"I don't think it was his idea," Ruth replied, joining her friend in laughter. "He acted gracious enough about it, but something told me he was following orders."

Their conversation turned to Patch and Ruth told all about her dinner with him the previous evening. "And I was worried about you," Karen remarked cheerfully. "I must be crazy. You're being ushered into private dressing rooms, and you're dating one of the handsomest Dodgers. I think I'm going to bed."

"Me, too," Ruth said, turning serious for the moment, "but I'm really glad you waited up for me. Say, that reminds me, I bought a couple of dresses in San Diego. Do you want to see them?"

"I sure do," Karen responded, getting up. "Come on,

83

show them to me."

Later, Ruth couldn't help thinking how lucky she'd been to meet Karen and to room with her. She had more in common with Karen than she had with any Dodger, including Patch. Ruth fell asleep, dreaming of a time when other women would be playing for the Dodgers. The road trips would be a lot more fun then.

11

The Dodgers' second home stand started with a three-game series against Montreal. Ruth found herself on the bench for the series, but on the night of the last game, Tommy told her that she would be starting the next day against Philadelphia, the leader of the Eastern Division. "Get a good night's rest," Tommy told her, "or the Phillies will send you home early. They're a tough team."

Ruth didn't need to be warned about the Phillies. She'd been studying their lineup, looking forward to the day she'd pitch against them. They had the heaviest-hitting team in both leagues. Pete Thorn, their first baseman, had been an All-Star for about 20 years. Kirby Witt, on third, could knock a ball out of any park in the league. Each of their outfielders was a dangerous hitter, and their pitchers, led by Steve Marlton, were among the best in the league. Pitching against the Phillies was going to be a real challenge for Ruth. Just hitting against them was going to be a challenge for her teammates.

"I'll be there tomorrow," Karen proudly announced that night. "A guy at school named Jeff asked me to go with him."

"Is he nice?" Ruth asked, wondering if her friend was starting a new romance.

Karen blushed slightly. "He seems nice," she said, "and he's terrific looking. I was surprised that he asked me."

"Don't put yourself down," Ruth said. "He probably thinks he's lucky to get a date with you."

From what Karen had been told, she and Jeff would be sitting somewhere behind first base in the lower deck area. Ruth promised to look for them. "Maybe I'll invite him here after the game," Karen said. "He probably would like to meet you."

"That'd be nice," Ruth replied and then turned her thoughts to the Phillies' lineup.

It was hot the next afternoon and Ruth halfway wished the games were being played at night. The sun felt good, but it burned up energy and Ruth was going to need a lot of energy to get by the Phils. In her warm-ups, she used an easy motion and didn't bother to test her fastball. "No sense in throwing your game in practice," Charley told her. "It's going to be a long, hot day out there."

When the umpire called, "Play ball," Ruth raced out onto the field with her teammates. "Take your time," Ernie called to her from behind the plate, tossing a new ball to her for the last-minute warm-up pitches.

Ruth dried her pitching hand on her pants leg and then did the same with her glove hand. Before putting on her glove again, she worked the ball with both hands, hoping to get some of the smoothness off its cover. Her few warm-up pitches went where she wanted them to go, and though she already was wiping perspiration from her forehead, she felt good.

Pete Thorn led off for the Phils. Looking in at him, Ruth remembered his batting stance from the time she'd watched him on TV when she was a little girl. His legs were bent slightly, and he seemed almost like a cat getting ready to spring. This is it, Ruth thought, as she went into her windup. Like a cat, Thorn jumped on the pitch and lined it into center field for a clean single. What really surprised Ruth was Pete Thorn's speed. He made a wide turn at first and she stepped over to back up the throw into second. The Dodger shortstop took the throw and faked a toss to first. Thorn hustled back to the base and Ruth moved back to the mound.

Glancing over at first, Ruth saw that Thorn was grinning at her. It was a friendly grin. "Good hit," she called, and he winked as if to say "thanks." Ruth wasn't embarrassed. The man had over 3,000 hits in his long career so one more off her wasn't a big thing. Keeping him from scoring was what counted, and Ruth made a few quick tosses to first to keep Thorn from leading off too far.

The next Philly also went after Ruth's first pitch, but all he could manage was a bouncer out to the mound. Ruth fielded the ball and whirled toward second. Her shortstop was moving toward the bag, but so was Thorn. Ruth turned and fired to first for out number one.

Again Ruth glanced at Thorn. He had called "time" after his slide into second, and he was dusting off his uniform.

"Good move," Ruth's third baseman called to her as she went to the rosin bag to dry her fingers.

"No batter," her first baseman called, and the Phillies'

center fielder stepped into the batter's box.

Working carefully, Ruth ran the count to three balls and two strikes. From her position, her next pitch seemed to catch the inside corner of the strike zone, but the plate umpire called it a ball and waved the batter to first base.

Tommy came charging out of the dugout to dispute the call. He was mad, and "blind" was one of the nicer things he called the umpire. As the discussion went on, Ruth guessed that Tommy was on the brink of being ejected from the game, but kicking the dirt and receiving cheers from the Dodger fans, he returned to the dugout.

Kirby Witt next stepped into the batter's box. He was big and his practice swings made him a menacing figure. Ruth couldn't afford to walk him, and she couldn't afford to give him anything too good to hit. She looked back at Thorn taking a short lead off second base, and from the corner of her eye, she saw some pitchers beginning to warm up in the Dodger bullpen. Wiping more perspiration from her brow, she looked in for the signal.

Witt was fooled by Ruth's first pitch and missed it for a swinging strike one. The Dodger infielders were in a few steps, hoping for a possible double play ball, and they let loose a full barrage of chatter.

"Way to go, Ruth."

"Let's get two."

The Dodger fans added their approval when Ruth's second pitch, a slow curve, caught the outside corner for a called strike number two. Ruth tried to waste the next pitch, but Witt wasn't taking any chances and he fouled it into the dirt.

A high "ball" followed, making the count one ball and two strikes. Ruth shook off her next signal, opting instead for a fastball. It went wide of the plate and the count was even at two and two.

This time, Ruth didn't attempt to second-guess her catcher. She pumped once and tossed up a big curve. Witt was waiting for it, and he hit a screaming line drive toward the left side of the infield. Turning, Ruth saw Larry Linden, the Dodger shortstop, make a leaping catch. The force of the hit knocked him to the ground, but he held on, rolled and flipped the ball to the Dodger second baseman. Thorn, who was moving with the hit, had no chance to get back to the base. It was a double play. The inning was over, and the Dodger fans were on their feet applauding Linden's magnificent fielding play. "Nice play, Larry," Ruth called to him when they reached the dugout steps.

"Lucky," he called back.

When Witt batted again in the fourth, he got hold of one of Ruth's fastballs and sailed it deep into the center field seats. No one was on, but his home run gave the Phils a 1-0 lead.

In the bottom of the sixth, the Dodgers fought back. Two singles followed by a long double into the right field corner pushed two runs across, and Ruth went back to the mound for the seventh inning with a one-run edge.

Leading off and hoping to rally his team, Thorn dropped an almost perfect bunt down the first base line. Ruth came off the mound fast and managed to scoop up the ball as Thorn raced by. Turning to throw, she saw that Thorn was in her line of fire. She tried to throw inside of him, but the toss pulled the first baseman off the bag and Thorn was safe at first. A few seconds later, the "E" for error blinked on the scoreboard. Ruth had made her first big league error, and from the look on Thorn's face, she could tell he was hoping the bunt would be scored a hit.

Ruth managed to get the next two batters, but a slow grounder by the second one pushed Thorn over to second base. He was in a good scoring position, and Kirby Witt was stepping into the batting box.

Calling "time," Tommy ran out to the Dodger catcher. After a few words, the Dodger manager returned to the dugout. As Ruth guessed, she was given the signal to walk Witt. As she lobbed the four pitches outside Witt's reach, the sprinkling of Philly rooters in the stands booed. Ruth felt the same way. She had wanted to pitch to Witt.

The next Phil popped out to right field and the top of the seventh inning was over. Though Ruth still wished she could have pitched to Witt, she couldn't fault Tommy's strategy. She'd gotten through another inning and was six outs away from beating the Phillies.

A solo homer by Goose Gandler in the bottom of the seventh pushed the Dodgers lead to 3-1. The additional run bolstered Ruth's confidence and she set down the Phils in order in the eighth.

The Dodgers didn't fare any better in their half of the eighth. As the team headed back onto the field for the ninth, Charley said, "Just get three more, Ruth."

"I will," she responded confidently.

Ruth felt good. Her arm was still strong and her breaking pitches were going where she wanted them to go. As she rubbed the baseball and looked in at the first

Philly batter, she knew she could finish the game as a winner.

Two outs later, Pete Thorn stepped up to the plate. This time, Ruth matched his grin. Pitching with all she had left, she ran the count to two and two. Thorn was swinging on the next pitch, but Ruth's fastball steamed right by him. It was Ruth's ninth strikeout of the game. It was all over. The Dodgers had topped the Phils, and Ruth heard the cheering as she raced for the dugout. She felt great until she saw the look on Patch's face.

"Good game," he said. "I'm happy for you even if it doesn't show."

"What's the matter?"

"Bad news," he said. "Can you meet me at Luigi's?"

"Sure," Ruth replied, "I'll be there as soon as I can."

As Ruth walked to her dressing room, she realized she hadn't spotted Karen and Jeff in the stands. She also realized she probably wouldn't get home soon enough to meet Jeff, but that could wait. Karen would understand. From the look on Patch's face, he really needed to talk to a friend.

12

Ruth didn't have to think hard to guess Patch's bad news, but she hoped she was wrong. She wasn't. "I'm going back to the minors," Patch said, as Ruth settled into a seat in Luigi's.

"I was hoping it was something else," Ruth replied. "When did you find out?"

"Before the game today. I'm catching a plane late tonight and joining the Dukes in Salt Lake City."

Dukes was the nickname used by Albuquerque. "You'll like Albuquerque," Ruth said, trying to cheer him. "I liked it."

"Don't spread it too thick," Patch said. "I know it isn't the end of the world. It's just a disappointment."

"You were doing pretty well, I thought. Was it Tommy's idea?"

"They just bought up the contract of some guy in the Mexican League and they're bringing him up right away. He's supposed to be a really heavy hitter," Patch explained. "Tommy told me he would have kept me if he didn't have to make room for this guy. He did say that he thought I'd be back next year, so I guess that's something."

"You will be," Ruth said. "The Pacific Coast League is only a jump away from here. You may be back before the season is over. You never can tell."

"Yeah, but I'm not going to bet on it. The only good thing about it is I'll probably be playing every day. How are the guys there?"

"They're good guys," Ruth said, "but you're going to have to get used to Bucky Weller, the manager. I thought he had it in for me, but after a while, I found out he was nasty to everybody. He's a good manager, though. By the end of the year, I sort of liked him."

"You mean you didn't hate him so much?" Patch asked with a chuckle.

"You got it," Ruth said, "and I'm glad to see that grim look come off your face. It doesn't suit you."

They were interrupted by several people coming over to their table to congratulate Ruth on her victory over the Phils. Because of Patch's sad news, Ruth felt slightly embarrassed by the attention, but Patch smiled across the table at her to show he wasn't feeling sorry for himself.

When the fans had departed, they each ordered a full dinner. "I'm going to miss this place," Patch remarked after their waiter had walked off.

"So am I," Ruth said. "I've only been here with you."

Patch started to respond, but for some reason, he stopped. For a moment, he sat there staring at Ruth. Then he reached across the table and held her hand. "I'm going to miss you, too," he said. "Lately, I'd been trying to think of a way to turn our friendship into something a little heavier, but I guess that'll have to wait until next year."

"How come?" Ruth said, teasing him a little.

"One of the guys gave me the telephone number of what he said is the prettiest woman in Albuquerque," Patch replied jokingly, "and you know a player always does better in his home ball park."

Ruth laughed. "Now there's something you must have heard in the locker room," she said. "I hope before I'm through that more women get into pro ball. Then we'll have our own locker room and some cute little sayings to pass around."

"I bet you will," Patch laughed.

After dinner, they sipped their coffee and sat around for a while, but Patch had to pack and get to the airport. "My treat," he said, slapping some money on the check. "You buy when I return."

In the parking lot behind Luigi's, they hugged each other. "I'm really going to miss you," Ruth told Patch and pushed him toward his car. "Now get going. You have a plane to catch."

Driving home, Ruth thought of all the little things she hadn't asked. What was Patch going to do with his car? Who was going to arrange for his mail to be forwarded? Did he have to return his Dodger uniforms? She stopped the string of questions, realizing she was thinking more like a mother than a friend. Patch would get by.

Karen seemed cheerful enough when Ruth walked through the door. "I'm sorry I couldn't come right home after the game," Ruth mumbled. "Did Jeff come over?"

"Yes, he did," Karen replied, smiling. "I think he

really came to meet you, but we had a pleasant dinner and he asked me out again for Friday. So I'm not angry or anything, but tell me where you were? You don't look very happy."

Ruth settled on the couch and told all about Patch's return to the minor leagues. "Well," she said, ending her story, "if it happens to me, I hope I get more time to pack than Patch did."

"If it happens to you," Karen said, shaking her head in mock disgust. "You now have more wins than any pitcher in either league and you're talking like that. I'm sorry about Patch, but you can't get me to start worrying about you at this point."

Ruth laughed at herself. "You're right," she said. "You just ended my acting career, but you're right."

The arrival of Miguel Ramos from the Mexican League made news on the *Times*' sports page the next day along with a tribute to Ruth's pitching mastery over the Phils. Patch's departure was noted in a short paragraph at the end of the Ramos story. Ruth wished more could have been said about Patch, but she had read enough sports pages in her life to know better. All she could do was hope he did well in Albuquerque.

Four days leter, Ruth dropped a game to the Mets. She held them scoreless for six innings, but they came alive in the seventh and shelled her with four straight hits. The last one was a triple, and when Tommy came out to the mound, Ruth couldn't argue with his decision to change pitchers. An off night, she told herself, but she wasn't happy with her performance. The loss put her record at 6-2.

Despite Ruth's loss, the Dodgers were climbing in the standings for Western Division leadership. They were in second place, only one and a half games behind the Giants. The other division teams were almost as close, so although it was still early in the season, it looked as if no team could be called a favorite to win the title.

The next day there was a break in the Dodger schedule, but instead of giving the players a day off, Tommy called them in for a brief practice. Ruth had been avoiding Maury, and he had been doing the same. That morning he had other ideas. Ruth was in the outfield fielding grounders when Maury moved in alongside of her. "Well," he said, "you really messed up things for that kid."

Ruth couldn't imagine what he was talking about, but from the look on his face, she guessed he was looking for trouble. "I'm not interested," she answered.

"You should be," he shot back. "That kid was a pretty fair ballplayer and he shouldn't have been shuffled off to Albuquerque because of you."

Turning and staring at him, Ruth said, "Just what are you talking about?"

"That kid Patch," Maury replied. "You and he were pretty chummy and that scared the front office, according to what I hear. The big shots forced Tommy to drop the kid."

Ruth laughed in his face. "That's about the stupidest thing I ever heard," she remarked. "Go tell it to one of your friends, if you have any."

"It isn't so stupid," Maury replied. "A hot romance between the lady pitcher and another team member wouldn't be good for the Dodgers and it wouldn't be good for baseball. The kid should have used his head. There are plenty of good-looking girls around, and not one of them ever thought about playing baseball."

Ruth had heard enough, and though she probably should have walked away, the idea never entered her mind. Her charge at Maury caught him by surprise and she knocked him sprawling with her gloved hand. Ruth didn't hesitate. She jumped on top of him and was throwing rights and lefts when several players came racing over and separated the two of them. The red marks on Maury's face told her that she'd been on target with some of her punches. "Turn her loose," Maury said. "I don't have to take this kind of garbage from her."

At that moment, Tommy arrived on the scene. "This is beautiful," he said in disgust. "The both of you get to my office right now and on the way there, don't start again. I won't put up with any more fighting. I promise you that."

Drained of most of her rage, Ruth just felt embarrassment. She wasn't sorry about what she had done, but she wished she hadn't done it in full view of the whole team. She followed Maury to the manager's office, moving slowly enough to keep a good distance between them. Halfway there, Charley fell in step with her. "What started it?" he asked.

"Later," Ruth replied, realizing that Maury might well create another story and make the matter his word against hers.

When they reached his office, Tommy motioned Ruth and Maury to take seats and then said, "All right, what started this thing between you two?"

"I started nothing," Maury said. "I was telling her a little tip about throwing a curve, and she said that she didn't need any help and jumped me."

"That's a rotten lie," Ruth blurted out.

With a slight twinkle in his eye, Tommy said, "That's what I was thinking. She jumped you because you tried to help her, Maury? What do you take me for?"

"Listen," Maury said, "I didn't start any fight. We had a few personal words. What they were doesn't matter. They weren't any good reason for her to jump all over me."

"Is that about it?" Tommy asked Ruth.

Ruth didn't know what to do. Even if she told exactly what had happened, the matter wouldn't really be over. Back in Union City, the rule she'd grown up with had been "fight your own battles," and it had been a rule for both girls and boys. Maybe it was the right rule. She didn't know. A knock on Tommy's door interrupted her thoughts. It was Goose Gandler. "Didn't you hear I was busy?" the Dodger manager asked.

"Yeah, I heard," Goose answered, "and I'm usually one to mind my own business. I'm making this an exception."

"Get on with whatever you have to say," Tommy barked at him. "I'm anxious to get to the bottom of this mess."

"This guy," Goose said, pointing at Maury, "has been pushing Ruth for a while now. I saw them almost get into it a week or so ago. Anyway, when we were changing this morning, he was hinting about some hanky-panky between Ruth and that kid Patch who got sent down. I didn't like it and the other guys who heard it didn't like it either. So I'm just putting that on the record."

Ruth was amazed. Goose had always acted friendly toward her, but she never would have guessed he was going to do what he had just done. She glanced at Maury. His facial expression showed some hatred for Goose, but his eyes showed something else. It was fear.

"Thanks for letting me know," Tommy said, and Goose turned and left the office.

"Were those some of the personal words you were sharing with Ruth?" Tommy asked Maury.

"Yeah," he replied, "that's right. You know, I've been in baseball for a long time. I started on sandlots when I was a little kid. I love the game, but I never figured it was going to end up like this. A great team like this doesn't need any girls. You must know how I feel. It's like being part of a sideshow."

Tommy shook his head in disgust. "You'd better go back to practice, Ruth. Maury and I are going to be here a while, but before you go, I want you to hear something."

Turning back to Maury, the Dodger manager said, "Back in the forties, it was a sideshow, too. Guys with small minds like yours didn't want any blacks to play baseball. For a short time, those guys did their little sideshow things, but decent people decided it was a game for Americans—white and black Americans. Now, with Ruth, we're making another change, and before you start telling me, let me tell you—you have a right to your opinion. Guys like you always know a lot about your own rights. Well, Ruth has a right to play and the talent to back up that right. Your rotten opinion can't change that!"

Tommy stopped and stared hard at Maury. Ruth got up

and backed out of the room. Instead of returning to the playing field, she went to her dressing room. She wasn't sure if it had been Tommy's speech or just an emotional release for all of the events, but she was crying and couldn't stop it.

13

That evening, Ruth went over to Sally and Charley McGraw's home for dinner. Charley had given her the invitation in the late afternoon. Ruth accepted after Charley told her that he knew most of what had happened with Maury and promised that the dinner conversation wouldn't be a rehashing of the events.

At dinner, Charley reminded Ruth that she would be in New York the following week for the start of the Dodgers' first Eastern road trip. At the beginning of the season, the trip had been uppermost in Ruth's mind. The fact that she'd almost forgotten it didn't bother her because she realized she'd settled into her new job and surroundings. Still she couldn't help wondering how she'd feel when she saw Mike again. She missed him, but not as much as she thought she would.

For the next few days, Ruth consciously tried to steer clear of Maury. For some reason, and she guessed it was her fight with Maury, her Dodger teammates seemed friendlier than ever. Maury avoided her, too, but his sullen appearance told her that he wasn't looking for any way to improve their relationship.

Ruth's seventh win turned out to be a two-hit shutout of the Giants, and the victory threw the Dodgers into a tie for first place. The *Times* called the game "Marini's best pitching performance," but Ruth wasn't sure that she agreed. Some sparkling fielding plays by her teammates had robbed the Giants of hits, and several of those batted balls could have gone for extra bases.

The Giants bounced back the following day and ended the Dodgers' home stand with a 9-4 win that gave the Giants a one-game lead in the West. It was a close race, but both teams were thinking about Atlanta. The Braves were red hot. They had an eight-game winning streak going for them and they were sitting two games out of first. Though the season hadn't reached its halfway mark yet, it promised to be exciting right to the finish.

By questioning Charley, Ruth learned she'd probably be pitching the Dodgers' second game against the Mets in New York. So she put in for three tickets to the game. Mike and her mother would be coming along with Mr. Levy, Ruth's boss when she had worked at the insurance company. In talking with Mike, Ruth had learned that an army of schoolmates from Union Hill High would be there, too, and though Mike wasn't sure, Ruth guessed that Mr. Schwenk, her high school coach, would be on hand. The thought of performing before old friends didn't frighten Ruth, but as the night approached, the pressure mounted.

With all that was happening to her, Ruth had just about forgotten the strange letter she had received. Her father was as far from her thoughts now as he had been during most of her life.

Ruth didn't see Mike during her first day in New York. He'd offered to drive over to her hotel that night after the game, but Ruth, though disappointed, didn't know when she'd be returning to the hotel. A reporter from the *Post* was doing a story about her and Charley and meeting with them after the game. The reporter turned out to be a young woman who was on her first big assignment for the sports department, and Ruth tried to help her as much as she could.

Ruth had planned to do a little shopping the next morning, but the lobby of the hotel was filled with reporters, and to avoid them, she returned to her room. For the moment, the idea of being a celebrity didn't thrill Ruth.

Later that morning, Ruth agreed to one interview. It was for Union City's *Dispatch* and the reporter almost couldn't believe that he'd been given the opportunity. "If it weren't for Union Hill High School, I probably wouldn't be here," Ruth told the reporter. "Besides, I still like to think I live in Union City."

The reporter didn't share Ruth's love for Union City. From his questions, Ruth gathered that he was as interested in LA as he was in writing for the *Dispatch*. When he turned to the idea of writing a movie script of Ruth's life, she politely ended the interview. She had a game with the Mets to think about.

The team bus to Shea Stadium that afternoon was buzzing with a big rumor which Ruth found hard to believe. Maury wasn't on the bus, and the players were saying that he'd left the team and gone home. In a few days, he was supposed to announce his retirement from baseball. Though the players didn't like him, they realized that they'd lost a good pitcher if the rumor was true.

When Ruth climbed off the bus, she saw Charley waiting for her. "I'll walk you to your dressing room" he said, but Ruth could tell he had something other than being an escort on his mind.

As soon as they were out of the hearing range of the other players, Ruth said, "Is this about Maury?"

"Yeah," Charley said, "I figured you heard the rumor. Well, it's more than a rumor. He's quitting baseball. Tommy was going to try to trade him, and Maury decided he'd played on enough teams. He's retiring."

"I'm not sorry to see him go," Ruth admitted, "but I guess I feel a little guilty about it."

"This isn't any time to feel guilty," Charley admonished her. "You have a game to think about, and besides, you didn't ask Tommy to trade him. It was Tommy's decision. He's paid to make those kinds of decisions and I can tell you right now, he doesn't feel the least bit guilty. My guess is that Maury will say that his arm has been hurting and that he was afraid he couldn't help the team anymore."

"You mean he won't say a word about me?" Ruth asked.

"No," Charley said, grinning at the look of surprise on her face, "because someday he might want to coach or even manage a team in the minors. He's probably hoping that you'll be the first and last woman in pro baseball, but I figure he's smart enough not to bet his whole future on that. You watch and see. I'll be right."

Ruth grinned back. "I hope so," she said. "I really do."

"Go ahead in and get dressed," Charley said, patting her shoulder. "I'll see you on the field."

Just before the game started, Ruth spotted Mike, her mother, and Mr. Levy in the stands. They waved to Ruth and though she knew several TV cameras were probably following her every move, she waved back. Touching the bill of her cap would have been a more professional move, but she didn't care. Seeing them excited her.

Ruth also noticed an extraordinary number of girls in the stands. She wondered if the Mets had run some sort of special promotion to bring them out. As soon as she and her teammates had settled in the dugout for the opening inning, Goose Gandler jokingly called to her, "Hey, Ruth, it looks as if every girl in New York came to see you play tonight. The older ones are going to distract us guys."

"Not after you hear them boo you," Ruth joked back. "They probably came to see me lose."

"Well, make sure you surprise them," Goose shot back.

The Dodgers went hitless in the top of the first, and the Mets raced off the field to the sound of enthusiastic cheers from their fans. As Ruth made her way to the pitcher's mound, she, too, received some cheers but there were enough boos mixed in to remind Ruth that she wasn't playing at home. During her warm-up tosses, Ruth thought of the many times she'd come to Shea Stadium and watched games. A little chill ran up her spine and she quickly turned her concentration back to the game and the batter waiting for the signal to step up to the plate.

Three batters later, Ruth raced off the field alongside her teammates. At the end of one inning, the score was Dodgers 0, Mets 0.

The Dodgers managed to get a hit in the second, but again they failed to score. The first batter Ruth faced in the bottom half of that inning was Dave Springerman. He was the home-run king of the Mets and though he struck out a lot, he was dangerous. His weakness was swinging at very bad pitches, but he had the strength to drive even the worst of pitches out of any ballpark.

To prove that point, he slammed Ruth's first pitch, which was high and outside, into the upper deck on the foul side of the right field line for strike number one. Ruth's next pitch nicked the inside corner for strike number two. She followed it with a waste pitch that sailed way outside for ball one. Springerman seemed anxious, so Ruth tested him with another outside pitch. It was a mistake. He reached across the plate and ripped into the right field seats to the delight of his fans. Ruth stood there, watching him trot around the bases. She didn't know how she would pitch to him the next time he came to bat, but he wasn't going to see any outside pitches.

After striking out the next batter, Ruth managed to get the next two to ground out. The inning was over but the Dodgers were down 1-0. "That Springerman hits anything," Charley told Ruth in the dugout, "but the guys will get the run back for you."

Helped by a decent bunt from Ruth, the Dodgers more than evened the score in their half of the third. They pushed two runs across the plate and Ruth returned to the mound with a one-run edge. As she did, she spotted

Mike waving to her and this time, she just smiled, hoping he could see it.

Ruth set the Mets down in order in the bottom of the third, and her team scored another run in the top of the fourth. The Dodgers were leading 3-1.

When Springerman stepped up to the plate again in the fourth, the Mets' fans stood and cheered. Ruth had walked the first batter of the inning and the second one had gotten in on a fielding error. Another Springerman home run and the lead would go over to the Mets.

Ruth tried a tight fastball and Springerman fouled it into the dirt for strike one. Her second pitch was high, but the Mets' slugger went after it and sent a screaming line drive into the boxes behind third for strike number two.

Ruth waved off the signal for the next pitch. She didn't want to throw a waste pitch. She was hoping to catch Springerman letting the pitch go by. Finally, after she had shaken off two signals, the Dodger catcher gave her the call she wanted. Checking the base runners, she went into her motion and whipped a fastball right across the heart of the plate. As she had guessed, Springerman was caught napping. The ball slammed into the catcher's mitt and the Mets' slugger didn't even wait for the ump's call. He dumped his bat on the ground and walked off.

After the next batter grounded out, Ruth threw her second strikeout of the inning. She'd kept the Mets from scoring, and though their fans probably didn't like it, they cheered Ruth all the way to the dugout and didn't stop until she stepped out on the dugout steps and waved her cap.

Springerman came to bat again in the seventh after Ruth had set down nine Mets in a row. This time, he lined a hard shot to center field and it fell in between the Dodger players chasing it, giving him a standing double. A single through the infield followed, but the return throw caught Springerman in a rundown after he had taken a wide turn around third. Finally, Springerman was tagged out. The next batter went down swinging for out number three.

Over the next two innings, the Mets failed to bat one ball out of the infield. Ruth had notched her eighth win, and the cheering told her that she'd won a few more fans along the way. She imagined all of her friends from Union City were pleased. "A couple of friends of yours are waiting in your dressing room," Charley told her. "I gave permission for them to see you there because I didn't think you'd mind."

"Who are they?"

"Give yourself a surprise," Charley suggested.

After exchanging congratulations with her teammates and manager, Ruth hustled off to her dressing room curious about the visitors. They were Mr. Schwenk, her baseball coach from Union Hill High, and Mr. Miller, the Dodger scout who had recommended her. Ruth was delighted to see them. They were proud of her and though they didn't stay long, they made her feel very good.

Mike was waiting when Ruth rushed out of the players' gate. They hugged each other before moving along to the spot where Mike had parked. Ruth told him about her visitors, and he told her about the many people from

Union City who had been at the game. Ruth's mother and Mr. Levy were waiting by Mike's car. Both of them hugged her and praised her pitching effort.

"You look great," Ruth told her mother once the four of them were seated inside the car.

"You do, too," Mrs. Marini replied. "I was worried that you might not be eating enough."

Ruth laughed. "You're a wonderful mother," she said.

"And you're a wonderful daughter," Mr. Levy remarked. "You made your mother famous in Hudson County. People stop her on the street all the time now and ask about you."

"Is that true?" Ruth asked.

Beaming proudly, Mrs. Marini said, "It really is. They want to know all about your record and the games you're playing—all kinds of things."

Ruth glanced over at Mike. She wished she could be alone with him and wondered how that might be accomplished. Winking as though he had read her thoughts, Mike said, "Your mom and Mr. Levy want me to drop them off in Union City. Then you and I are going out before I return you to your hotel. I thought you might be interested in grabbing something to eat in one of our old hangouts."

"Is that okay with you?" Ruth asked her mother. "I don't want to run out on you and Mr. Levy."

"It's fine with us," her mother answered. "Now tell us how you struck out Springerman. The people at work are going to be asking me all about that tomorrow."

"Me, too," Mr. Levy added.

Ruth talked on about baseball until Mike reached Ruth's

old neighborhood. "Just leave us off on Bergenline Avenue," Mrs. Marini directed Mike. "We're stopping for donuts and coffee."

Ruth climbed out of the car and kissed her mother. "I'll call you," she said, and her mother hugged her tightly.

"Drive carefully," Mr. Levy told Mike. "You have valuable property riding with you."

"Don't worry," Mike joked. "If anything happens, your insurance company will hear about it."

Ruth laughed, thinking Mike was the same as ever. A little later, she had a different thought. They were both trying, but something had changed. They were seated at a table in the Clam Broth House in Hoboken. They'd just finished eating a bucket of steamed clams and were waiting for some iced tea. Finally, Mike said, "I heard you were dating some guy on the Dodgers."

Surprised by the remark, Ruth asked, "Where did you hear that?"

"I didn't really hear it," Mike admitted. "I read it in one of the sports columns in the *News*. It wasn't any headline story."

"It sure wasn't," Ruth said, grinning across the table, "but I'll tell you all about it."

Mike listened, but when Ruth had finished telling about Patch, he said, "Hey, you didn't have to go into all that. I don't own you."

Ruth frowned. "I know," she responded. "I was just trying to let you know that I miss you a lot."

Ruth wasn't sure what kind of response she expected, but she didn't like it when Mike changed the subject. She wished she wasn't separated from Mike for such long periods, but she knew there was nothing she could do about that. Even if they got married sometime in the future, she wasn't leaving baseball. She smiled to herself at the thought of marriage. It was ridiculous.

They rode back to New York without much talk passing between them. When they reached Ruth's hotel, Mike said, "I have to get home. I have to start work at about five tomorrow morning."

Ruth was disappointed, but she hid it. "We're leaving after the game tomorrow night," she said. "Are you still planning to come to LA for your vacation?"

Turning to her, Mike said, "Yes, I am. I know I haven't been much fun tonight, but this being apart bothers me. I feel like we have to get to know each other again every time we see each other. Anyway, I miss you and if it doesn't show, it's just because I'm stupid at times."

Ruth kissed him long and hard. "I'm stupid, too," she said. "I should have been telling you I wanted you to come to LA rather than asking you about your plans. Now you hurry up because I'm counting the days."

They kissed once more and Ruth climbed out of the car. It was late. The streets weren't deserted, but the few people on them seemed to be in no hurry to get where they were going. Ruth waved to Mike and turned toward the entrance to her hotel. Like the people passing by, she wasn't in a hurry. Too many days were going to pass before she saw Mike again and too many things were happening in her life. She pushed open the hotel door and stepped inside. The sound of some familiar voices reached her ears, and she spotted some of her teammates gathered on a couch in the lobby. "Hey, Ruth," one called, "come on over here. Where have you been? We're still celebrating."

Ruth smiled and hurried over to them. It was nice to be on a team, and it was especially nice to have friends on the team.

14

The following day, the Dodgers announced Maury's retirement, citing continuing pain in his throwing arm from bone spurs and calcium deposits in his elbow. In interviews, Maury went along with what the Dodgers had said. One reporter told him that there were rumors that he'd had a running battle with Ruth Marini, but Maury laughed that off. "She's a damn good pitcher," he'd told the reporter.

The newspaper reports amused Ruth and she had to admit that Charley had come close to forecasting all of them. She'd learned something from the event that seemed to be a rule of pro baseball—team matters weren't public matters. And she didn't hear one player question the stories about Maury. This silent understanding amazed her.

Between the road trip and the Dodgers' first week back in LA, Ruth picked up 3 more wins without a loss. She had 11 wins to her credit, and in both leagues, only Dick Sanchez of the Yankees topped her with 12 victories. The LA sportswriters were beginning to say that she was a sure thing for the National League's Rookie of the Year Award—the same title that Jackie Robinson had won in his first year in baseball. One writer even suggested that she could win the Cy Young Award, an honor that had been won by only one other rookie pitcher—Fernando Valenzuela. Ruth tried hard not to think about the awards, but the stories swelled her pride.

One important thing on Ruth's mind was the All-Star game. It was a week away and scheduled to be played in Anaheim. Luke Quinn, the manager of the Cincinnati Reds, had been selected to lead the National League stars. At the beginning of the season he had been quoted as saying that he didn't think Ruth could make it in the National League. He had probably changed his mind, but so far, he hadn't named the pitchers he would use and some writers were speculating that Quinn would bypass the Dodgers' female star. Ruth wanted to pitch in the All-Star game, and the reporters tried to get her to say so. "It's up to the manager," she wisely answered. "I don't pick the pitchers and there are a whole lot of good ones in this league."

Five days before the All-Star game, Luke Quinn called Ruth and told her that he wanted her on the pitching staff of the National League All-Star team. After Ruth hung up the phone, she laughed at herself, realizing that she had thanked him about six times. Still she was overjoyed. She called Mike, her mother, and Charley with the news. Mike and her mother congratulated her. Charley did the same, but he added some advice. "Do the best you can, but don't try to do any better than that," he said. "We have a lot more games to play, and if you hurt your arm, you're not going to be much help to us."

Charley went on to tell her how an injury during an All-Star game had cut short the pitching career of the great Dizzy Dean. Then he started another story, but Ruth assured him that she'd gotten the point.

The following day, Tommy congratulated her and started in on the Dizzy Dean story. Breaking in, Ruth related the story to him. "I guess you get the point," he said, "but I still hope you strike out a few of those American League bums. I'll be rooting for you."

Except for pitchers, the players on both All-Star teams were selected by the votes of the fans. In being chosen, Ruth joined three Dodgers who had been voted onto the team. Her friend Goose had received the most votes of any player in either league. "Congratulations," he told Ruth, "I'm glad you made it."

"I still can't believe it," Ruth answered, and she meant every word.

She also received a brief note of congratulations from the Dodger owner. "I'm sure that every person in the Dodger organization would join me in congratulating you," it read. "We're proud of you. You're a richly talented individual, and I'm the luckiest owner in baseball." It was signed "Gene Webber."

When Ruth returned to her apartment that evening, she was tired but happy. It had been a long day, full of excitement and anticipation. As she walked from the parking lot to the building entrance, she noticed a taxi parked at the curb with its lights off. The driver got out as Ruth approached and came slowly toward her. He looked a lot older than the man in the picture her mother had sent, but Ruth recognized him. It was her father.

Ruth's face became tense, and she stood up very straight. Looking steadily at the man, she spoke in a low voice. "I don't think I want to talk to you."

The man nodded his head sadly. "I didn't think you'd know me by sight," he said, "but I did want to get a close look at you."

"I've changed a lot since you last saw me," Ruth said abruptly as she began to move toward the apartment door again. "I have to go in."

"Please don't go yet. I only want a couple of minutes of your time. I don't want anything else. I swear."

Over the years, Ruth had dreamed about something like this happening, but the man standing in front of her didn't look anything like the man she had imagined. In her imaginary meetings with her father, he had been young and handsome, and he had taken her and her mother away with him to a beautiful, big house. The man standing awkwardly before her was middle-aged and ordinary. Dressed in a rumpled driver's uniform, he looked tired and rather sad. Her father wasn't a figure from a childish daydream. He was very real. Ruth waited to hear what he had to say.

He groped for the words. "I saw you pitch last week. I watched the game on TV. I was real proud of you."

Ruth kept her eyes on his face, but she made no reply.

"Okay," he continued, "I probably don't have any right to be proud of you. I know that, but you can't do much about feelings. They come on you even if you don't have a right to them. Can you understand what I mean?"

"Did you ever think about how I felt?" Ruth responded.

Her father studied the ground at his feet. "In the beginning I did," he said, "but after a while, I stopped thinking about your mother and you. I was out of your life, and you were out of mine. Then this baseball thing came up. When I saw your picture and read about you in the newspaper, I could tell that you'd grown up all right. I guess I just wanted to see for myself. I'm sorry if I've bothered you. I don't know what else to say."

"I don't know what to say either," Ruth mumbled. "I think I should go."

"Yeah, it's late," her father replied. "Thanks for letting me talk a little."

"I have to go," Ruth repeated.

"Take care of yourself," her father whispered as she stepped around him. "Take *good* care of yourself."

Ruth kept walking, but she had a sick feeling in her stomach. She was walking away from her father, and she would probably never see him again. Much of the anger she had kept inside her had been washed away by their meeting. Now she was not angry, just sad and sorry. Sorry for him and for herself as well. Without looking back, she hurried into the apartment building.

Karen was still up, but Ruth had already decided not to mention the encounter with her father. "You don't look too good," Karen said. "Is something the matter?"

"Not really," Ruth answered, fighting off a sudden desire to tell Karen everything. "Some guy cut me off on the freeway, and I guess I got a little scared. Other than that, I'm just tired."

They talked a little while longer before Karen told

Ruth to go off to bed. "You really look like you need some rest," she said.

Minutes later, Ruth climbed into bed and sat propped up on her pillow. She could not sleep, her mind was so filled with thoughts of the past. She remembered all the good times she and her mother had shared. She also thought of all the times she had wished for a father. Her wish hadn't come true, but aside from that, her life had been very much the same as the other kids with whom she had grown up. She even remembered hearing her friends complaining about their fathers and thinking that maybe she was lucky not to have one.

Ruth thought about the man she had met outside her apartment building. Her father. How strange it had been to see him after all these years. She did look a little like him, she knew that now. While she was growing up, she had imagined him far away, living a life of ease and wealth and pleasure. Now that she had met him, she realized how wrong she had been. Whatever had happened to her father over the years, his life had not been any better or easier than the life she and her mother had led.

Ruth wondered what had happened to cause the look of sadness on his face, but she didn't think she would ever find out. She didn't expect that her father would try to see her again, and she didn't think she would ever look for him. But Ruth knew he would always be part of her life, even if they never met again. Whenever she looked in the mirror, she would see the reflection of his tired, sad face in her own features.

Ruth reached for the lamp on the night table and switched it off. She realized that she would probably never tell her mother what had happened, and she wondered what painful secrets her mother had kept from her over the years. Ruth imagined that adults were better than kids at keeping secrets. Well, she was an adult herself now, with a secret of her own to keep.

15

In the next few days, Ruth was so busy with preparations for the All-Star game that she had little time to think about the meeting with her father. She was very proud to be on the All-Star team, but she never guessed how much attention she was going to receive. Reporters from all over the United States and from several other countries hounded her for interviews. A woman being selected for the All-Star team during her first year in the big leagues was more than just an ordinary news story. Writers doing articles for magazines also competed for some of her time.

The constant attention bothered Ruth, but she realized that the reporters and writers were only doing their jobs. She tried to be fair to all of them, and most of them were understanding when she needed to end an interview.

The many companies that wanted to use Ruth's name on their products or have her appear in a TV ad were something else. Ruth had no idea how to deal with these people and she finally asked Charley for his advice. "You're going to need an agent or some kind of business manager," he said. "I'll check around and get the names of a few of them. Then you can talk to them, but just wait until after the All-Star game. You have to sign a contract with an agent or business manager, and there's no sense in getting tied up with someone you might not like."

Ruth followed Charley's advice, informing one company representative after another that she would have her agent get in touch with them. One company she didn't put off was the chewing gum company that gave away baseball cards with their gum. Being on a baseball card wasn't going to make her rich, but the thought of some kid trading a Hank Aaron or Nolan Ryan card for a Ruth Marini gave her a big thrill.

On the morning of the All-Star game, she drove to Anaheim Stadium for a practice and get-together with the team. In a way, she expected some of the players to act as Maury had acted, but most of them were friendly and the few who seemed less than friendly gave no real sign of disliking her. One fact was clear. The players were honored to be on the team, even the ones who had been on it many times, and they were going to play as hard as they could to win. Ruth promised herself that she'd do the same.

That afternoon, Luke Quinn called Ruth aside and informed her that she'd be starting for the National League. "Horse Hansen is our starting catcher," he said, "so you make sure you go over the signals with him. I'll be giving them to him from the bench. Now tell me how you feel."

"Wonderful," Ruth replied, thinking that her answer probably wasn't quite right for a baseball player, "and my pitching arm is okay, too."

A smile spread across Quinn's face. "You just pitch three wonderful innings," he said, tapping her gently on the shoulder. "I don't want any of those guys on that other team saying that the American League is too tough for a woman."

"I hear you," Ruth said, smiling back at him.

Horse Hansen caught for the Reds, but in his first few years in the big leagues, he'd played for the Red Sox. Because of that, he was able to give Ruth some valuable tips about some of the batters in the American League lineup. For his last bit of advice, he said, "Just remember there are no really bad hitters on an All-Star team and no really bad pitchers. So don't make any mistakes and hope that the guys behind you don't make any. If there aren't any mistakes, we walk off winners."

Ruth respected Horse, but his last piece of advice amused her. She had heard the same advice back in Little League, but she had learned not to take it too seriously. Perfect pitches sometimes got knocked out of the ballpark. Luck, she had discovered long ago, deserved some credit in any victory. Horse probably believed in luck too, but he couldn't tell that to a young player.

A sellout crowd poured into Anaheim Stadium that night. Karen and Jeff were there, using the complimentary tickets Ruth had passed on to her roommate. Ruth had also given tickets to Charley and Sally McGraw. She had a general idea where the four of them would be sitting, but after running her eyes over that area, she gave up the attempt to spot them.

When the public address announcer called out Ruth's

name and she ran out to join the other starting National Leaguers standing and facing the crowd along the baseline in front of their dugout, her body was tingling with excitement. She didn't know from experience, but she couldn't imagine a World Series being any more thrilling. The air seemed almost charged with some weird kind of electricity. "Tip your cap," the player next to her said, and she realized the fans were still cheering for her.

She watched as the American League starters were called out onto the field. She'd played against some of them in exhibition games, but others she knew and admired only as a fan. She fought off the strong emotional response she felt about seeing them now and pitching to them soon. Tomorrow, they could be her heroes again, but tonight she had to stop them cold.

Next, many All-Stars of the past were called out on the field. As their names were read and they came out waving to the cheering fans, Ruth joined in the applause for the great old stars. The National League oldtimers lined up alongside the National League team, but before that, they went from player to player shaking hands. Ruth was thrilled to meet every one of them. One of the last ones to be announced was Charley McGraw, and the Dodger fans in the crowd climbed to their feet and cheered. Ruth was delighted, even though she felt slightly embarrassed for not knowing right away that Charley would be called. "You'll be doing this someday," he told her, "and believe me, it's easier than playing."

Ruth smiled, fighting off the urge to hug Charley. His funny little remark eased some of the tension, though she still felt somewhat awed by the old stars. A moment later, she took off her cap and joined in the singing of the National Anthem. A soft breeze played on the flag and Ruth couldn't help thinking she was lucky to have been born and raised in the United States. She remembered how her history books in school had called it "the land of opportunity." It was, she thought, as she struggled to keep in tune with the anthem.

When the singing was over, Ruth and her teammates hustled back to their dugout. The American League stars moved out to their positions, and the loud applause of the crowd indicated the game was about to start. Ruth slipped on her warm-up jacket and joined in the chatter to encourage the National League's first batter.

Two pitches later, a long fly fell into the glove of the American League center fielder for out number one. "Good try," Ruth called when the first batter returned to the dugout, and several other players made similar comments.

The next two batters also hit fly balls, but both were caught, and the National League stars moved onto the playing field with a "0" on the scoreboard for their first effort.

Ruth took her warm-up pitches, and for the last one, she whipped over a fastball. "They can't hit one of those," an infielder called. "An easy out at bat," said another. Then she stepped around the mound, smoothing out the playing surface to fit her pitching stride, while her infielders tossed the ball around and the umpire signaled for the first batter to step up to the plate.

Lenny Gonzales tossed off one of the two bats he'd been swinging and positioned himself in the batter's box.

Gonzales played second for Oakland, and he was the fastest base runner in the major leagues. Ruth's infielders moved forward a few steps, hoping to stop Gonzales from bunting for a base hit.

On her first pitch, Ruth caught the outside corner with a sharp curve for strike one. Her second pitch went wide, but Gonzales faked a bunt before letting it go by for ball one.

The Oakland All-Star was swinging at Ruth's third pitch, which was a fastball. He missed, making the count one ball and two strikes. Ruth came right back with a fastball on the inside corner, and the umpire called it "strike three." Gonzales didn't like the call. He turned to the umpire and exchanged a few words with him before returning to his dugout.

"Two more like that," an infielder called to Ruth, and the others picked up the chatter.

Now Paul Hroncich, Minnesota's great first baseman, stepped up to the plate. Ruth had pitched against Hroncich in a spring exhibition game and knew he was especially tough on fastballs. But Hroncich wasn't waiting for a fastball. He lashed out at Ruth's slow curve and fouled it into the upper deck on the third base side.

The plate umpire threw a new ball to Ruth and she rubbed it while looking in for her signal. It was for a fastball, and for a moment, she thought about shaking off the signal. Then she remembered the signals were coming from the bench and decided not to try to second-guess the Reds' manager. He proved to be right because Hroncich was looking for an off-speed. Caught off guard, he swung late and missed the fastball for strike number two.

Again the signal called for a fastball and Ruth concluded they hoped to slip a third strike past the Minnesota star, who would be expecting her to waste a pitch. Hroncich realized his mistake, but the best he could do was make a feeble swing. He tipped the ball into Horse's glove for strike number three and out number two. "Next time," Hroncich called to Ruth before striding angrily off to the dugout.

Batting in the number three slot for the American League All-Stars was Doug Dreier of the White Sox. Dreier was batting .348 in regular season play and leading the American League in runs scored. He was in his fourth year of big league play, and he'd made the All-Star team in each of the years. Ruth had never faced him, but Horse had warned her that he was a low-ball hitter.

Pitching carefully, Ruth fell behind with two high throws to Dreier who stood in there patiently waiting for the low pitch he wanted. He got it on Ruth's next pitch, but all he could manage was a foul into the screen behind the plate for strike one.

Next Ruth caught the inside corner for strike two. Dreier didn't like the call and he passed a few words with the plate umpire, while Ruth's infielders shouted words of encouragement to her.

Horse called for a curve, and Ruth broke off a beautiful pitch. Dreier started after it and changed his mind—too late. In his effort to pull back, he let go of the bat and it flew from his hand. Ruth saw it coming and tried to jump out of the way, but she wasn't fast enough. The bat caught her on the shin of her right leg.

Ruth fell to the ground and rolled over in pain. Dreier

was the first player to reach her. "I'm sorry," he said, kneeling beside her. "It slipped."

"I know," Ruth replied, trying not to give in to the unbearable pain she was feeling.

Along with players, the National League trainer and a doctor on call rushed out to the scene. Ruth could feel the tears running down her face, but she couldn't stop them. She'd never felt as much pain in her life. "Let's get the ambulance out here," the doctor said. "I think it's a fracture."

"It hurts a lot," Ruth whispered to him.

"I know," he replied. "I'm going to put a temporary splint on it and give you a shot for the pain. You'll be all right."

Ruth wanted to believe him, but the pain was making her dizzy. A few seconds later, she fainted. When she awakened, she saw Charley McGraw staring down at her. "What happened?" she said. "Where am I?"

"You passed out," he replied, "and as you can see, we're riding in an ambulance. I figured I should ride along because I never taught you how to field bats."

Ruth smiled faintly. "You're right," she told him.

Ruth's leg didn't hurt as much as it had, but Charley explained that that was probably because of the shot she'd been given. He continued talking, telling her about little injuries he'd had and making little jokes about them. She hurt, but she was glad she wasn't alone.

At the hospital, x-rays were taken of Ruth's leg before she was moved into a private room. "Hey," Charley said, looking down at her in the hospital bed, "this is better than a hotel room."

Ruth reached out for his hand. "No, it isn't, and I'm sorry I made you miss the game."

"They always come out the same way," he answered, smiling at her. "One team wins, and the other team loses. I'll bet on that."

Ruth didn't answer. She felt sleepy, but she wasn't sure she'd be able to sleep with the dull, aching pain in her leg. A man came into the room. "I'm Dr. Fine," he told Charley. "Ms. Marini has a fractured tibia. We're going to put it in a cast. It's nothing to worry about, but we're going to keep her here for a couple of days to be sure of the setting."

"Did you hear that?" Charley asked Ruth.

"Yes," she replied, thinking about how long she'd be out of action.

A few minutes later, a nurse and an orderly arrived to wheel Ruth off to have her leg put into a cast. Charley looked down at her and brushed a tear from the corner of his eye. He was sure she was going to be all right, but he didn't like seeing her in pain. "I'll be here when you get back," Charley promised, and Ruth smiled bravely.

16

When Ruth awakened the next morning, she realized she must have fallen asleep while talking to Charley. She looked at her splinted right leg raised in traction. It didn't hurt anymore, but it looked like a mess. She guessed that she looked like a mess, too, and wondered if she should ring for the nurse. She needed a comb and brush and other things.

A few seconds later, Karen walked into the room, carrying Ruth's hair dryer and a bag filled with what Ruth guessed were other toilet articles. "I came early because I thought you'd want these things," Karen explained. "I hope you don't mind."

"Are you kidding?" Ruth replied. "I'm glad to see you. I really need to get myself straightened up."

Just about the time Ruth had made herself presentable, Sally and Charley marched into the room. "I didn't mean to put you to sleep last night," Charley joked, "but tell us how you're feeling?"

"Fine," Ruth replied, glancing at her injured leg, "I really feel as if I could walk out of here right now."

"Well, that's out," Charley told her, "but I'm glad you're feeling better."

"Who won the game?" Ruth asked, changing the subject.

"The National League," Sally reported, "by a score of 9-2."

"You stole the show," Charley said, holding up the *Times* for Ruth to see.

The headline, in extra large type, read: MARINI FELLED BY WAYWARD BAT. The picture beneath the headline showed Ruth on the ground with a crowd around her.

"After we leave, you can read about it," Charley said, just as Ruth's breakfast was brought into the room, "but before that, we'll watch you eat."

They continued talking while Ruth picked at the eggs and other food on her tray. She was sure the food was good for her, but she didn't like the taste of it.

"By lunchtime," Sally said, "everything will taste better. You're just not hungry enough right now."

"Hey," Ruth suddenly said, "what about my clothes in the dressing room?"

"They're all being delivered to your apartment today," Charley replied.

A nurse came into the room with a thermometer in her hand. "Now how did you people get in here?" she asked. "Visiting hours begin at one except for emergencies, and Miss Marini isn't in the emergency category. You'll have to come back later."

Ruth said goodbye to her friends before she slid the thermometer under her tongue. She hadn't been awake for long, and she couldn't understand why she felt tired.

When the doctor arrived, the tired feeling was the first thing she asked about.

"The pain was a shock to your system," the doctor explained, "and besides, you're probably still feeling the effects of the painkiller shot into you."

He checked her pulse and asked her to wiggle her toes on the injured leg. "I'm going to put your leg on a pillow," he said, "but I don't want you to get up by yourself. I don't want you putting any weight on that leg. If you have to go to the bathroom or anything, the nurse will assist you. Later today, someone from physical therapy will come by and show you how to use the crutches."

"Crutches," Ruth repeated. "How long will I be on them?"

"I'd say three weeks," the doctor replied, "as long as you keep your weight off that leg. By the way, I'm one of your fans."

"You still are?" Ruth said, smiling. "Even though I didn't know enough to get out of the way of the bat?"

Dr. Fine smiled back. "Well, you tried. And at least you didn't get hit in the head."

Ruth fell off to sleep after reading the newspaper accounts of her accident and the game. She was awakened by the ringing of the phone next to her bed, and she was pleased to hear her mother's voice on the other end of the line. "I saw the whole thing on television," Mrs. Marini told her, "and I almost fainted. A few of the neighbors were watching with me and they said I was pale as a ghost. I talked to Mr. McGraw last night and he told me you're going to be all right. Do you want me to come out there?"

"No," Ruth replied, "I'm okay. I have a splint on my leg, but I feel fine."

They talked on and Ruth supplied as many details of the accident as she could remember. Finally, her mother said, "That man should be thrown out of baseball."

Ruth knew she was referring to Dreier and laughed. "Don't be silly. It was an accident. Next time, I'll move quicker."

"There shouldn't be a next time," Mrs. Marini answered. "You played all through high school without getting hurt."

"You're right," Ruth said. "There won't be a next time. I love you, so don't worry."

When Ruth put down the receiver a few minutes later, she felt good to have spoken with her mother, but she was also glad that her mother wasn't coming to California. She was old enough to take care of herself and if she needed a little help, Karen would be there. She didn't care if her mother eventually moved to California to live, but that would be a lot different than having her visit the apartment every day for the next couple of weeks or even sleep on the couch.

A little later, bouquets of flowers and plants began to arrive in her room. Some were from players on her team, some were from fans, and others were from players on other teams in both leagues. Two dozen roses came with a card from Doug Dreier. It read: "I'm rooting for your quick recovery, and I'm sincerely sorry."

After dinner, Sally called to say that she and Charley would be by the next day. They'd heard she was going to have a lot of visitors that night. Ruth asked her to pass that information along to Karen, so her roommate could skip the visit if she wanted.

A few minutes later, Tommy, Goose, and several other Dodgers came into the room. They were loaded down with boxes of chocolates and bunches of flowers. Ruth talked and joked with her friends for a long time. "When you get back," Tommy told her, "you're going to have to practice getting out of the way of flying bats."

"That sounds like fun," Ruth responded, and her teammates laughed.

A second later, Gene Webber walked into the room and surprised them all. "Let's not act shocked," he said cheerfully. "After all, I did help to get Ruth into this mess and she is one of my most valuable players."

"You sure did," Tommy joked. "I told you we should have signed Dreier last year."

They continued joking a little, but it seemed obvious the Dodger owner wanted to talk to Ruth, so Tommy and the others bowed out.

"I didn't mean to run them out," Gene Webber apologized and sat down next to Ruth's bed.

"You didn't," Ruth said politely. "I think they were about to leave just before you walked in."

"Well, that's good, and I'm glad to see you're in such good spirits. I could tell you were in a lot of pain on the field last night."

"I sure was," Ruth replied, "but I think I'll be out of here in a few days, and I guess I'll be pitching again in about a month."

"That's what I came to talk to you about," Gene Webber said, taking on a more serious look. "I think you and I are facing another big decision."

Ruth's stomach knotted up. She didn't know what he was getting at, but it didn't sound good. "Tell me," she said as bravely as she could.

Slowly and with much care, Gene Webber explained what he had learned about her fracture. It wasn't serious, and Dr. Fine had indicated that she probably could be pitching in about a month. They'd also discussed the dangers of going too fast with pitching, and Gene Webber had told the doctor about the experience of Dizzy Dean.

Ruth had heard the story before, but she asked Gene to tell her again what had happened to the great old St. Louis Cardinals' pitcher.

"He hurt a bone in his foot during an All-Star game," Gene Webber explained, "and by rushing things, he changed his pitching delivery. Well, he was never the same after that, and believe me, he had been one of the greatest pitchers in the history of baseball."

"So what do you want me to do?" Ruth asked, knowing pretty much what the answer was going to be.

"I'd like you to come back nice and easy. As of now, you're on the disabled list. I'm not going to keep you on it if you don't agree, but I was hoping I could talk you into letting the rest of this season slide by."

"Oh, no," Ruth protested, "I can't do that, Mr. Webber. Tommy is counting on me and so is the team."

"I know," he admitted, "I was, too, but you and I have more in this than the other guys. If you go back too soon and you aren't as good as you were, some people will blame it on your injury. Others will discount your injury. They'll say that you were just lucky in the first half of the season and that the batters were getting wise to your pitching. You'll be giving them the chance they want to say that women don't belong in the big leagues. Now I don't want that, and you don't want that."

"No," Ruth mumbled. She could feel the tears running down her cheek.

"I didn't come here to make you unhappy," Gene Webber said, gently touching her hand. "I'm really sorry."

Reaching for a tissue, Ruth said, "You go ahead and say what needs to be said, Mr. Webber. I'm all right."

He waited for her to blow her nose and rub her eyes. Then he said, "Ruth, a lot of people think that what we're trying to do is nothing but a silly experiment. When we started, we were more outnumbered than General Custer. You turned that around. We're winning now. Someday, maybe half of our team will be women, but that's going to take a lot of time. Right now, more young girls are coming out to our games, and I understand that many more are trying out for Little League teams. You're the reason for that. All I did was give you your proper chance. So, we're winning now, but you're going to need a couple of good seasons before we can say the battle is over. I'm just asking you to go slow and make sure you're able to give your best. I know I'm asking a lot, so why don't you think about it and talk it over with Dr. Fine?"

"I will," Ruth agreed. "I guess I owe you that much."

Gene Webber bent over and kissed Ruth on the cheek. "You don't owe me a thing. Whatever you decide along with the doctor, I'll be with you. Right from the beginning, you've been everything I thought you'd be. Now you take it easy and think about what I've said. Oh, and if there's anything you want, you be sure to let me know."

After Gene Webber left, Ruth switched off the lights in her room and cried her eyes out. She understood all of the points he had made, but she was tired of being the first woman in baseball and having to be better than any other rookie player. She didn't want to be the female Jackie Robinson. She just wanted to be a player, and she wished all the girls in Little League would get another hero. She was no hero. She didn't even have the good sense to get out of the way when a bat came flying at her.

In the morning, Ruth felt better. The sunlight poured through her window and reminded her how good her life really was. She reached out to her night table and lifted off a handful of cards that had come in the mail. One was from a little girl named Dolly Marion. She'd written "age eight" next to her name. The card read, "Hury up and get beter." Ruth hoped Dolly's spelling would get better, too. A lot of the other cards were from young girls, too, and Ruth couldn't help thinking she did owe them something after all.

As Ruth went through the stack of get-well cards, she found one that surprised her. It looked the same as many of the other cards she had received, but it was signed by her father—Frank Marini. Ruth slipped the card into the travel pack that Karen had brought to her. She would put it away with the growing collection of things she planned to keep.

That morning brought Ruth another surprise. Just as she was finishing breakfast, Mike walked into her room. "I took my vacation early," he explained before she had a chance to say a word.

Ruth reached up and pulled him down to her for a long kiss. When they separated, she looked into his eyes and said, "I missed you so much. If I had known you were going to come, I might have gotten hurt sooner. Anyway, I'm taking my vacation early, too."

When Charley and Sally walked into Ruth's room a little later, they found her kissing "somebody." When the somebody turned around and showed his red face, they were happy to see Mike. They had hoped he'd be able to make the long trip to California.

The three of them sat down and listened as Ruth told them a little about her talk with Gene Webber. Then she told them her decision. She wanted her friends to be the first to know. She was going to let the rest of the season slide by. Ruth liked using Gene Webber's phrase and she liked him. He was a kind and thoughtful human being.

When Ruth had finished, she studied the expressions on their faces. Their eyes were shining. They weren't disappointed because they really cared about her. "You'll be great next year," Charley said.

"She's great now," Mike said in a serious voice, keeping his eyes on Ruth's face.

"Well, she'll be even better next year," Charley replied.

Ruth smiled happily at her friends. "You know," she said, "I think you're right."

MEL CEBULASH grew up in an urban area in New Jersey much like the hometown of Ruth Marini, the main character in his series of sports novels, *Ruth Marini on the Mound*. Like Ruth, Mel played ball in high school, but he went on to become a writer and editor rather than pursue a career in sports. His many published works, both fiction and nonfiction, reflect his continued fascination with sports and his special interest in writing for young readers. The three novels in the Ruth Marini series combine the author's expert knowledge of baseball with an absorbing account of a young woman's struggle to become a professional athlete.

Lerner Publications Company
241 First Avenue North, Minneapolis, Minnesota 55401

Sports Story Collection

BOOKS DUE ON LATEST DATE STAMPED